Third Edition

The Key to Survival

Interpersonal Communication

Tracey L. Smith

Mary Tague-Busler

Lewis & Clark Community College

WAVELAND

PRESS, INC.

Long Grove, Illinois

For information about this book, contact:
Waveland Press, Inc.
4180 IL Route 83, Suite 101
Long Grove, IL 60047-9580
(847) 634-0081
info@waveland.com
www.waveland.com

A Dedication

This edition to *Key to Survival* we again dedicate to our mentor, colleague, and friend, Pat Goehe. We both consider ourselves blessed to have been taken under your wing. You taught us that communication is indeed the key to our survival. We owe you more than words can ever express. You remain our inspiration and guiding light. You showed us that teaching also means caring about your students as people. You taught us that a good teacher could offer students ways to learn new information and improve their lives while doing so. You helped us believe that when the world locked us out, communication skills were the key. We hope that our students will look back someday and believe that we have touched their lives in the same way that you have touched ours. Thirty years ago you began a plan to bring us together. Your vision was well founded. We thank you with all our heart.

We also dedicate this text to our daughters, collectively numbering four. Ashley and Jessica Smith and Nicole and Kelsey Busler, you are all we ever hoped for. You have all grown into fine young women. You remain our inspiration. We hope you look to us when the world seems overwhelming.

Contents

Preface   ix

1   An Introduction to Communication   **1**
Why Study Communication?   4
Why We Communicate   6
Communication Axioms   9
The Basics of Communication   13
The Communication Model   14
Conclusion   18

2   Verbal Communication   **19**
What Is Verbal Communication?   21
Uses of Language   22
Characteristics of Language   23
Our Misuse of Language   25
Suggestions for Effective
    Verbal Communication   28
Conclusion   30

3   Nonverbal Communication   **31**
What Is Nonverbal Communication?   33
Types of Nonverbal Cues   33
Uses of Nonverbal Communication   39
Characteristics of Nonverbal Communication   40
Difficulties with Nonverbal Communication   42
Suggestions for Effective
    Nonverbal Communication   44
Conclusion   46

4   Listening   **47**

What Is Listening?   49
The Listening Process   49
Nonlistening Can Be Troublesome and Costly   51
Why We Don't Listen   52
The Benefits of Learning to Listen   58
Becoming a Better Listener   59
Conclusion   62

5   Self-Concept and Self-Esteem   **63**

What Are Self-Concept and Self-Esteem?   65
How Is Our Self-Concept Formed?   66
Characteristics of the Self   72
Communication and the Self   74
Making Positive Changes   76
Conclusion   79

6   Self-Disclosure   **81**

What Is Self-Disclosure?   83
Self-Disclosure Is a Choice   84
Why Self-Disclose?   85
When We Choose Not to Self-Disclose   89
Characteristics of Self-Disclosure   90
Challenges to Self-Disclosure   92
Guidelines for Self-Disclosure   94
Five Steps to Effective Self-Disclosure   96
Conclusion   98

7   Gender Communication   **101**

What Is Gender Communication?   103
Why Are Men and Women So Different?   106
Problems with Gender Communication   114
Suggestions for Avoiding
    Cross-Communication   117
Tips for Effective Gender Communication   120
Conclusion   123

8   Perception   **125**

What Is Perception?   127
Primary Physiological
    Perceptual Influences   128
Secondary Physiological
    Perceptual Influences   130
Psychological Perceptual Influences   133

Characteristics of Perception   136
Challenges to the Perception Process   138
Decreasing Perceptual Misunderstandings   140
Conclusion   141

9   Defensiveness   **143**
What Is Defensiveness?   145
Defense Mechanisms   146
Defense-Producing and
   Defense-Eliminating Behaviors   149
Conclusion   154

10   Conflict   **155**
What Is Conflict?   157
What Contributes to Conflict?   158
Characteristics of Conflict   159
Conflict Styles   160
Approaches to Conflict   165
Conclusion   168

Epilogue: The Susan and Jason Saga   **171**

Glossary   173
Index   179

Preface

We are two ordinary people who have lives filled with successes and failures, much like you. We know that regardless of our life experiences, communication is the key that has helped us get through. Communication has enriched our lives and contributed to our successes both personally and professionally. We want to share our experience of communication with you in this text.

As you read this text, we want you to feel as if you are having a conversation with us. We have used our own personal anecdotes and experiences for this reason. We believe that you can learn more about communication if you can identify with the "real life" situations in which they occur.

We have introduced Jason and Susan to this text. They too are ordinary people with ordinary lives. Through their experiences communicating with one another, you will begin to understand the concepts of communication that we will be exploring throughout this text. You may even recognize behaviors that remind you of yourself at times!

We do not claim to know all the answers to interpersonal communication, nor do we offer an in-depth view of each concept. It is our goal with this text to offer you a simple, straightforward overview of interpersonal communication that you can directly apply to your own daily lives.

A textbook revision cannot be undertaken without the help of numerous people. We would like to thank our friends, families, and students for offering us the opportunity to learn from them. We thank our colleagues, especially Jeff Harrison, Wanda Hall, and Patty Morrisey for their suggestions and insights to clarify ideas in this text. To the people at Waveland Press, we express our gratitude for allowing us the opportunity to share our knowledge. To you, the reader, we thank you in advance for giving us the privilege of opening the doors to communication. We offer you the key to survival, communication.

An Introduction to Communication

Me, We, They—Who Must I Talk to Today?

CHAPTER HIGHLIGHTS

- Communication is essential to human survival.
- Communication satisfies four needs: physical, practical, social, and ego.
- There are several axioms (guidelines) that can help us to understand communication.
- There are five types of communication: intrapersonal, interpersonal, small group, public, and mass.
- Communication can be achieved in two ways: verbally and nonverbally.
- A basic model can help us to understand the communication process.
- There are several reasons why messages can be misinterpreted.

Jason was pleased with himself. He had been working very hard and finally felt like he had reached the top! He had the proof in his hands. He was holding the key to a company condo. He could not believe his good fortune. Jason remembered when he had taken this job right out of college. He had interviewed on campus with many prospective employers. He had gone from booth to booth and was feeling overwhelmed and depressed. No one seemed to be able to use his skills. Then he had stopped at Investco. The representative had been impressed with his resume. She also had said that he had good communication skills. Three years later, here he was, with the condo key in his hand. Once junior associates proved themselves with the company they were promoted to full associate and given full benefits. One of these benefits was free company housing. He couldn't wait to tell Susan.

Jason's thoughts drifted to Susan for a moment. He had met her three years ago as well. After he had left the Investco representative, he went to The Station. The Station was the" in" spot for college students and young business people. It served as a gathering place to network, wind down, and just have a good time. The atmosphere was professional, yet relaxed. Jason had stopped by there on that day to have a bite to eat. He had just ordered his meal when he saw her—Susan. She was standing a few feet away. Although Jason had never believed in love at first sight, he did at that moment. He tentatively waved, and to his surprise, she approached his table. They started a conversation and had been together ever since. Jason knew Susan was the woman he wanted to marry. He had wanted to propose for a long time. He had purchased a ring months ago, but had delayed asking Susan to marry him, because he did not want her to live in his cramped apartment on a junior associ-

ate's salary. He had been so busy lately that he and Susan had not had much time for each other, but now he was ready to tell Susan why he had been so uptight and how he really felt.

Jason smiled. The key in his hand was like a magic potion that would change all of that. He could propose and surprise Susan with a ring and the key. He would take her to the condo tonight and show her what would be their new home. Living in the condo would require a short commute by train for Susan to get to work, but she would love the train ride. Jason was excited because Susan loved surprises. He knew she would be pleased. He picked up his phone and began to dial her number.

Meanwhile, Susan had been experiencing a particularly difficult day at work. The project she had been working on had just taken a turn for the worse. She had been forced to call the client with the bad news, and he had not been pleased. She also had to suspend two employees for discipline infractions, and it was not even lunchtime! She kept reminding herself why she stayed at this job. She was trying to save enough money so she could afford a bigger apartment. She wanted to assure her boyfriend Jason that they could afford to be together. She knew her cramped apartment did not send a message of success. Susan thought about Jason for a moment.

She had met him at The Station three years age. She had been instantly attracted to him and thanked her stars for him everyday. Susan was ready to marry him, but she sensed that Jason was not ready to make a commitment. She was sure that Jason believed she could not adequately contribute to the financial resources necessary to be a couple. He was always asking her if she was happy in her small apartment, if she ever wanted to get something bigger. The way he asked, she knew he was hinting at something, but she could not figure out what. She wanted to tell him how she felt and that she wanted to share her life with him, but he had seemed so preoccupied lately. They had barely seen each other. In fact, he had just called her and told her to be at The Station by five—that it was very important and not to be late. That was all he had said. Usually they talked for a few moments, but he was very abrupt this time. She was worried. He had not seemed like his usual self. Oh well, she could not dwell on it right now; she had a project to finish. If she did not get it done, she would have to call Jason and tell him she could not make it by five. She didn't want to do that. Susan went back to work.

Jason arrived at the train station at half past four. He had stopped by his apartment to get the ring and had stopped at the florist to get a dozen red roses tied with a velvet ribbon. He had attached the key to the condo to the ribbon. He was all set! He realized that he would have to reveal the condo surprise as soon as Susan arrived, because the roses with the attached key would be hard to hide, but the ring and the proposal could wait until later. He hoped she said yes!

Susan was scrambling. How had the day gotten away from her? It was already four-thirty. She knew she had another hour of work at the least. She had to make a decision and make it fast. She would work for thirty more minutes, then call Jason on his cell phone and tell him she would meet him at quarter after five.

Jason watched the clock. He scanned the face of every arriving passenger. At quarter to five he began to get nervous, where was Susan? He had left his cell phone at the office because he had not wanted to be disturbed. Office communications could be so intrusive at times. He did not want any interruptions tonight. He wanted to focus strictly on Susan. Five minutes later he wished he had brought the phone because there was still no sign of Susan at the station.

Susan stopped working at five. She called Jason on his cell phone. His voice mail picked up and she left a message that she would be late. She hoped he would not be upset, he had sounded so strange today. She left the office, hailed a cab, and was on her way to The Station.

Jason boarded a train at five fifteen for home. Susan had not come. He wondered what had happened. Maybe she knew he was going to propose and wasn't ready to make a commitment. Maybe she had decided to avoid him. She had sounded very odd on the phone this morning. She had seemed mad and had spoken in clipped, abrupt tones. As the train sped away from the station Jason mourned his lost love and wondered what had gone wrong.

Susan arrived at The Station at exactly five fifteen. She went inside, got a table, and waited. At six Jason had not arrived. Something was wrong, she had known by his voice on the phone. He had been abrupt. He had stressed that she should not be late. He must have waited and then left. He probably wanted to break up with her. He must think she was not worth the effort. Susan paid her bill, walked outside, and hailed a cab. On the ride home from The Station, she mourned her lost love and wondered what had gone wrong.

Why Study Communication?

Stop! That's right; the first thing we want you to do now is quit reading and think for a moment. The preceding story has nothing to do with you right? You may wonder what a mushy love story is doing in your college textbook. Or, you may feel sorry for this couple and wonder why they did not tell each other how they felt before things went wrong. No matter what your opinion about the story, all of us have been in a situation similar to that of Jason and Susan. We have been victims of miscommunication at some time or another. We use communication to get through our day, to express our opinions and our emotions. We would be lost without it, yet sometimes communication goes astray. Most likely we've experienced more breakdowns in communication than we would have liked. A simple misunderstanding like meet at "the station" versus *The Station* can often have major repercussions.

So what use is a *class* in communication? You may be thinking that since you already know how to talk, you know how to communicate. Although talking is a very important part of the communication process, there are many other elements as well. The various elements that we use to communicate are all learned skills that work together in a very complex process, allowing us to express ourselves to others. This process is essential to human survival. Therefore, it is important to learn about how this process actually works. That is why you are here, taking a communication course—so that you can learn the elements necessary to communicate effectively with others.

What will you gain that will make you feel the class has been a worthwhile learning experience, one that contributes to a more fulfilling life? We believe that this will be one of the most vital courses you will ever take. You will not only learn about communication, but you will also learn and practice skills that will help you become a more effective communicator. As your communication becomes more effective and you find that your relationships and interactions with others improve, we hope that you will agree with us that this course is indeed essential to your survival. Although you have been communicating from the time you were born, there is still much to be learned. Everyone can benefit from improving communication skills. Misunderstandings occur all too often, as we saw with Jason and Susan. Misinterpretations of voice tone and volume or words can all dramatically alter our messages to others.

The ability to communicate well will be important your whole life. Communication helps us come together as families, tribes, and nations. We must master the skill of communicating to function effectively in society. Doctors, teachers, managers, workers, parents, children, husbands, and wives all need to communicate to get through their day. You communicate from the time you get up until you go to sleep at night. Even if you are not talking with another person, you may be thinking thoughts in your head. This is also a form of communication.

Even though it is something you have already been doing, you must re-evaluate your communication techniques from time to time, add new skills, and perfect others. The development of our personal communication skills is an ongoing and very important process. We want to help you learn skills so that you will not be in a situation such as Jason and Susan's. We will examine many different types of communication, as well as explore the process of how we communicate to see how we might succeed or fail in this process. Let's first examine the reasons why we communicate.

Why We Communicate

For centuries, humanity has relied on the power of communication to express basic needs, fears, joys, and frustrations. What would you do if you couldn't communicate with others? What if you had no means of expressing your needs, feelings, or thoughts to another human being? What if there were no way to talk, no sign language, no expressions, or no other means to connect with others? Think about that scenario for a few moments. It is likely that such a situation would be very uncomfortable. Having no interaction with others would create a vastly different world. In fact, communication is so important to us that without communication with others we would probably not survive—the role communication plays in our actual survival is most significant.

There are four survival needs that we share as human beings: physical needs, practical needs, social needs, and ego needs. Each one can be satisfied through our interaction with others as well as through our own internal thought processes and conversations we have with ourselves. To understand communication's important role in our survival, let's examine these basic needs.

Physical Needs

Starting in infancy and continuing throughout our entire lives, we seek to satisfy our physical needs. Such needs include air to breathe, water to drink, and food to eat. If these basic needs are unmet, we cease to live. We would survive for only a matter of minutes without oxygen. We can exist without water for only a few days, and lack of food will lead to our death in less than a month. Obviously, physical needs are of critical concern to each of us. So what role will communication play in the fulfillment of these needs?

While it is true that people can exist and have their physical needs met without communication with another single human being, they cannot meet their needs without self-communication. You must communicate with yourself in order to monitor and understand your physical needs. When you feel hungry, you tell yourself to eat. When you are thirsty, you talk to yourself about what you want to drink. Ignoring these need messages that your body transmits can lead to illness or even death. People with eating disorders like anorexia and bulimia stop eating because, as these diseases progress, their internal self-communication becomes flawed, and they ignore the calls for food from their body.

For most of us, there is a need for communication at a higher level as well. We must translate our self-communication into communication with others to satisfy our needs. We ask for or buy food; we say we are thirsty; we see a doctor when we experience shortness of breath. In addition, most of us pay for necessities rather than raising and growing food, digging a well, or treating our illness with medicinal roots and herbs. This means we need a source of income, which means a job. A job means communicating on a regular basis with others. Communication is necessary at many levels to satisfy our physical needs.

Practical Needs

Once our physical needs are met we turn to those needs that help us meet the reasonable demands of our daily routines. For example, we remind our child to wear a sweater; we ask our teenager if she needs lunch money; we tell our spouse to have a good day; we call the office to ask for messages. All of these seemingly simple, mundane tasks require communication with others. However, we must also be aware that many practical needs are also met through communication within ourselves, as when we make a mental note to pick up the dry cleaning or buy paper towels on our way home from work. Therefore, discussing daily routines, performing tasks, or giving commands helps us meet very practical human needs. In these situations, we often balance our needs with those of other people. Societal functions lead us to the next level of needs, social needs.

Social Needs

As humans we live together in organized groups; we live in a **society**. We interact within these groups and need to function socially or affably together. We therefore have social needs that we fulfill through our relationships with others.

People cannot live alone. Most of us need companionship and affection. We need to know that we are cared for and loved. We seek approval as children and continue to feel the need for acceptance throughout our lives. This type of need absolutely requires communication with others. There is no way someone can communicate his affection without using some form of communication. While it is possible, but unlikely, that the first two needs can be met through self-communication alone, social needs can't be met without communication with others. Skill in communication is essential in social situations because we must concern ourselves with the needs of others as well as our own needs. To have a friend we must be a friend, and that means communicating. When a friend comes to me with a problem, I must sometimes forsake my own needs to listen to my friend. Empathy, sympathy, caring, and love are all social needs whose fulfillment is made possible through communication.

Looking at our society as a whole, we see that although there is hunger and homelessness in America, most people are meeting their needs at the physical and practical levels. Unfortunately, the same is not true of social needs. When people don't have their social needs met, the quality of their lives is severely affected. They often take out their frustrations through anger directed at others. In order to exist peacefully with others in society we must learn to be effective communicators and encourage others to be so as well. Lack of effective communication is one of the most significant factors in contributing to conflict between and among people.

Many people never fulfill their social needs. They fail to communicate their need for approval and acceptance. In this way, we look to others to define who we are. These people's opinions of us help us to determine who we are and how we feel about ourselves. Social interaction helps us to form a sense of self, or ego. This brings us to the fourth need that we have as humans, ego need.

Ego Needs

Along with social needs we have the need to achieve a feeling of positive self-worth. The development of a positive sense of self-worth requires effective communication with others. Through socialization we discover ourselves. The relationships we develop as we fulfill our social needs help us to reveal, define, and clarify ourselves as individuals. Positive social interactions allow us to feel good about ourselves; negative interactions often make us feel inept. Effective communication is essential if we are to feel like worthwhile members of society. Meeting ego as well as other needs through communication is our key to survival.

From this discussion you can see why this text is named *The Key to Survival.* Communication is not just a tool to express ourselves or a process used in forming relationships. It isn't just an amusing way to pass the day. Communication is *essential* to our survival as human beings. The needs we have, even to exist physically, are dependent upon communication. Therefore, we must learn as much as we can to become effective communicators.

Our investigation will take us into many areas of our experience and we urge you to be open in sharing problems you have communicating. Sharing our experiences aids us and others in understanding these problems so that we may attempt to resolve them together. Sharing can help us to avoid future problems, and it can make relationships stronger. One observation we have made over the years of teaching communication is that although the names and circumstances change, the problems that exist with communication remain constant. By discussing these common problems, we can find solutions. We can find, by sharing our experiences, what went wrong and can offer suggestions to improve these circumstances through the use of more effective communication.

Much of what is contained in this text will not be new to you. You have experienced it, maybe on a daily basis. You may not recognize the technical terms, but you will recognize the situations and circumstances. That is why learning about communication is so important. You are already doing it, will never stop doing it, and will benefit from doing it better! It is a process that we can't avoid. We have even established a network of communication vaster than any other system prior to this time called the Internet, greatly expanding our ability to communicate with others all over the world. Our lives will always depend on communication. It truly is the key to survival. Therefore, let's establish some basic guidelines to help us understand it better.

Communication Axioms

Before we continue, let's propose some guidelines that will set a framework for our study of communication. These guidelines are statements that we will accept as the truth, or **axioms** of communication. The following axioms will provide us with a basic idea of this complex process of transmitting and exchanging ideas that we call communication.

Communication Takes Work

Many people who take this course believe that having the ability to communicate effectively can solve all of their problems. First of all, **interpersonal communication,** the act of two people communicating face to face, is a mutual activity. It is between and among people, not one person against another. A person should gain as much from an exchange of thoughts and feelings as she contributes. Therefore, the ability to be an effective communicator is a wonderful thing, but in order for communication to go smoothly, both people have to be highly skilled. If one person is not skilled, or communicates poorly, then miscommunication can occur. Misunderstandings can and do result. Therefore, communication interactions can often create problems, not solve them. Remembering that communication takes work can help you become better skilled. The willingness to make a conscious effort can help keep misunderstandings at a minimum.

Communication Is Not Good or Bad

There are problems that can occur when we are communicating. Was my message clear? Was my message received in the spirit in which I intended? Did I come away from the exchange with a positive feeling? You may think that such questions imply a value judgment, leading us to believe that our communication is either good or bad. This is simply not true. Our messages are either effective, meaning the other person understands, or they are ineffective, meaning the other person is confused. Good or bad is not the point. Remember Jason and Susan. Susan had a very frustrating day at work. Nothing she did that day seemed to turn out right. When Jason called she was up to her elbows in frustration. Needless to say, the conversation was clipped and resulted in Susan and Jason believing that the other was angry or upset. This was ineffective communication; good or bad doesn't apply, and such a value judgment doesn't fix the situation.

While you may be tempted to focus on this as a bad situation, try to look at the communication overall and see where it went wrong. In other words, looking at communication to find out what led to what, what worked, and what didn't, is a more objective and effective way of learning than judging the situation as good or bad. Later we'll discuss some of the reasons why the results of communication are not always positive, as well as the communication skills that could have been used to make communication effective. For now, it is enough to understand that Jason and Susan's communication was ineffective.

Communication Takes Time

In our pressed-for-time world, with fast-food restaurants, microwave ovens, and instant access to the Internet, we want everything now. It would be wonderful if we could offer you a quick, easy way to be a better communicator. However, effective communication takes time. We are inclined to become impatient with anything that takes too much time. The average television show only needs 30 to 60 minutes to resolve any form of conflict, from trying to fit a large family into a small house to finding a long lost relative. You can visit a bookstore and find a book that teaches you how to fix anything or do anything better in 30 days or less. Yet real life is very different. Try instructing a child of two not to touch the stove. This is a very important and time-consuming lesson. The child's safety is at stake; however, the child sees the stove as something new to explore. An adult must explain time and time again why it is important for the child to avoid the stove and not touch it. This requires an explanation of the concept of hot and cold, and may even require an experiment with temperature. The adult must give the child, who lacks the experience of danger and its outcome, an understanding of why he is being told not to touch, another time-consuming process.

Most people are usually quite understanding if they are given appropriate information and *time* to digest new facts. Adults, as well as children, need time to understand new ideas. All too often we assume that since it's simple and logical to us, others will comprehend a new idea the same way and in the same amount of time that we do. This is not always true. Therefore, time is often necessary to clarify messages, and therefore all communication takes time.

Another reason that effective communication may take time is that you will be learning new skills and unlearning old ones. While it is true that you have been communicating all your life, you may find that some of your communication behaviors are ineffective and need to be changed. When our students try a new technique, they sometimes state that it doesn't work. "How long did you try it?" we ask. "All weekend," they say. "How long have you been doing it the other way?" "My whole life," they answer. Obviously you cannot unlearn in two days what took 20 years to learn! The "old way" has been developed, experimented with, and reinforced for a long time. A *new* skill, whatever it is, takes time to understand and learn, and it takes a much longer time to consistently use that new skill. The first time you were on ice skates, you were probably a little wobbly, but you kept at it, and finally you were able to circle the rink without falling. The same is true of communication skills; with increased confidence and practice you can master them, too. They just take time.

Communication Is Dynamic

In many ways, an investigation of the process and techniques of communication is an attempt at the impossible. We can never take a "slice" of an effective conversation and look at it under a microscope to see what has happened. We can never duplicate that process in the future. No two situations are exactly alike. Even one short communication encounter changes from second to second during an exchange. Our emotions change. We process information differently. We react with and to others. We can analyze these situations and get an idea of the *probability* of a method being effective or ineffective in communication, but we can't guarantee that what worked once will work again. There are too many uncontrolled and variant factors. Communication is dynamic because it is always changing and those who are participating in it are always changing too.

Communication Is Essential

Every day we are in situations involving people with whom we have problems. For example, you aren't happy at work. You could quit and find another job, but usually this alternative is not practical every time you become frustrated with your boss or colleagues. You've had a fight with your mother. You could move out, but financially that may not be a feasible alternative. Many people tend to remain in stressful or uncomfortable relationships rather than seeking solutions. Our emphasis in this book remains on finding what went wrong with the communication in the first place. By studying both parties in the conflict and finding out how a misunderstanding occurred, most people can find ways to work out a problem. With time, skill, and desire, the quality of our communication in the relationship can be improved. Once our communication interactions are improved, the relationship can often survive and thrive. Our mission is to learn the skills needed to deal with the issues that lead to misunderstandings. Why did my brother blow up when I asked to borrow his car? Why did my instructor react so angrily when I asked why I didn't get credit for an answer on the test? These are problems that can be resolved. Using effective communication to deal with these kinds of issues can help us improve the quality of our relationships. We learn to understand ourselves and others more objectively through effective communication.

Communication Is a Mutual Process

The communication process usually involves another or others; it is mutual. However, the only person who can control what you think, say, or do is you. The only control you have in the communication process is how and what you choose to say. You have no control over how someone else reacts to your words, and you have no control over what others say. You *can* create a situation in which you attempt to influence another person, but you cannot make that person do what she doesn't want to do. Others can, and do, influence, teach, punish, and reward us to get us to react the way they want us to, but it is our decision, within our control only, to ignore or attend to their wishes. Therefore, communication is a mutual process, with all parties involved responsible for their own interactions in the process.

We ask you to take responsibility for your actions and words. We ask that you understand that what and how you say things has an effect on others. We also ask that you let go of any notion that you can make someone feel, think, or do what you want him to do. We must take responsibility for our own behavior and stop believing we can make others behave the way we wish. Trying to make others do as we wish can lead to ineffective communication and strained relationships. We must also learn to let go of the belief that others can make us do or react in some way. We are ultimately in control of our own actions.

Communication Is a Learned Skill

Since there is no magic wand, and communication is dynamic, you find yourself in situations in which you react spontaneously. It is better to carefully choose an appropriate response. Perhaps you may even have to postpone talking about a situation until later, or you may have to agree to disagree. Learning communication skills provides you with options so that you can use the method that is best suited to the situation. If any response were appropriate for all circumstances, there would be no need to study how to be a more effective communicator. We believe that the ability to communicate effectively is a learned skill, and a valuable one at that. With practice and perseverance, you can create a vast arsenal of tools to help you in all communication situations—especially when conflicts arise.

The axioms above will serve as reference for our future discussion about communication. Keep them in mind as we try to define and explain the basics in the complex process of exchanges with and between people that we call interpersonal communication.

Activity for Further Understanding

Why Communicate?

In this activity you will examine your understanding of the purpose of communication and why it is so essential as a key to our survival. Your class will need to assemble in small groups to discuss and record the following:

1. Write your group's definition of communication. Don't go to the dictionary or the glossary of this text for this definition. Create it from ideas discussed by your group members. Arrive at a consensus for your definition. Write it down.

2. After deciding what communication is, answer the question "Why do people communicate?" Make a list of reasons; have everyone contribute their ideas.

After all groups have completed the first two steps, each group shares its conclusion with the rest of the class. Discuss any similarities and/or differences between group definitions and purposes.

The Basics of Communication

If we, as your authors, are to communicate effectively with you, the reader, throughout this text, we need a basic understanding of the words we will use consistently in our study. Since we like to practice what we teach, we'll start with what we asked you to do in the previous exercise. Here is *our* working definition for communication: **Communication** is the process of thinking and feeling and receiving and conveying messages to ourselves and others in a manner that brings ideas and people together. There are categories of communication. For example, if communication is the process of thinking and feeling, then our internal beliefs and emotions are our self-communication. We talk to ourselves in our head; we have memories, ideas and experiences that are stored in our brain. We generally have several of these thoughts swirling around in our head at any given moment; this internal communication is called **intrapersonal communication.** When we share our thoughts with another person, we are engaging in interpersonal communication. There are three categories of interpersonal communication, each dependent on the number of people with whom you are communicating. For example, when a third person joins the conversation, and then several more (to include up to 20 people), you are now engaging in **small group communication**. If you are speaking to a roomful of people, you are in a **public communication** interaction, and if you are sending a message to thousands of people, then you are doing **mass communication**. Therefore, no matter how many people are involved, the process is the same.

There are a few characteristics we need to introduce that will become the tools we use to discuss the process of communication. We can communicate through verbal and nonverbal means. *Verbal communication* refers to spoken or written language, whereas *nonverbal communication* refers to any communication that does not use language, but instead uses body movements or appearance, space, or voice tone, to name a few of the elements involved in nonverbal communication. These elements will be explored further in the next two chapters. For now, it is enough to realize that the process of receiving and sending messages occurs verbally, nonverbally, or uses both. Communication also requires the ability to listen. Most people confuse listening with hearing; however, *listening* is the psychological process of attempting to understand a message. *Hearing* is simply the physical process of sound waves striking the eardrum and signaling the brain that a message has occurred. We hear a great deal more than we listen to. The process of listening is so important that we will devote an entire chapter to the topic later in the text. For now you need to understand that when we use the words *listen* and *hear*, we mean two different processes; the physical one (hearing) is necessary for the psychological one (listening) to occur.

The Communication Model

Finally, we would like to clarify the communication process by showing you a simple model of communication. A model is a simplified representation of a more complex process or concept. This model attempts to freeze the communication process so that you can see what is happening. Remember, communication is dynamic and ever changing, so this model is merely representative of what actually happens. The process cannot really be frozen. However, by looking at a simplified model we can see the nature of the elements involved in the process. We can then use that as a guide in understanding the process overall.

Experiences have happened to us from the day we were born. These experiences are stored in our brain and have a role in creating who we are—our personality. These experiences shape how we think and feel. In communication we call these collective experiences our **personal environment.** In order to communicate effectively with someone else, we must isolate those experiences that relate to what we want to convey to others. This is necessary to help us form a message that another person can understand. When we experience a thought, we do not initially think it in words, but experience it as a mental image. This is the first step in sending a message: you (*communicator 1*) have an idea, opinion, or feeling that you want to share with someone else (*communicator 2*). For example, let's say you want to ask someone to have coffee with you after

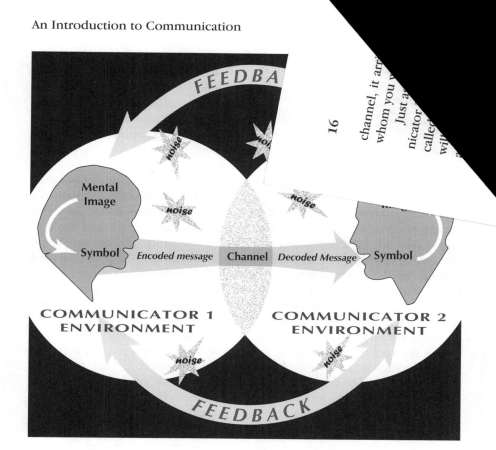

class. The beginning of this idea occurs with your mind "seeing" an image that represents you and your friend sharing that coffee break. The process of turning your mental image into something that others can understand is called **encoding.** You choose **symbols** (i.e., words and/or gestures) that are also shared with communicator 2 to present your image. Once you have encoded your image, you have created a message. A **message** is simply the idea you want the other person to understand. You are now ready to deliver this idea or message to communicator 2. You must choose how you wish to deliver your encoded message. That message must travel through some medium or **channel.** Therefore, the channel is how the message gets there, and there are many types of channels. For example, a channel may be visual, such as a gesture that is seen, or vocal, such as spoken words that are heard. It can also be a combination of the two. Will you speak, gesture, or both? You might express the invitation for coffee by smiling and saying, "Dale, would you like to go have coffee after class?" In this case, you have used a combination of channels: vocal, verbal communication, and visual, nonverbal communication, a smile, in a face-to-face encounter. Once the encoded message travels through its

ves at its destination, communicator 2. This is the person
ant to understand what you are attempting to communicate.
communicator 1 turns a mental image into a message, commu-
2 must turn the message back into a mental image. This process is
decoding. Once communicator 2 has decoded the message, he
attempt to respond. This response is called **feedback**. Dale may
nswer the invitation to have coffee by saying, "I would love to." He has
provided feedback to you, communicator 1.

While this may appear to be a linear process, (the message originating
with communicator 1 and ending with communicator 2), the process of
communication is really more of a circular process. This is because both
communicators are simultaneously sending messages back and forth to
each other. All behavior is potential communication; as long as we can
see another person, her behavior sends us a message. We are constantly
getting signals, or messages, from others. This constant exchange of messages, whether verbal or nonverbal, is the element that makes communication a dynamic process. The process represented in this model is the
same whether you are speaking to one or several people.

In a communication exchange, the message sent (encoded) is not
always the message received (decoded). Let's say you want to describe a
square to another person. You encode and send your message, but when
the other person receives and decodes it, his mental image is of a rectan-
gle, not a square. Obviously the message received was not the message
intended. There are three reasons why this error can occur.

1. ***The sender and receiver do not share personal environments.***
   When the communicators do not share environments, messages go
   astray. Personal environments include experiences such as educa-
   tion, religion, home atmosphere, historical background, emotions,
   and so on (represented on the diagram as a circle around each communicator). No two people share exactly the same personal environment. We are all unique individuals, although our environments can
   overlap in certain areas. Sharing environments helps us to better
   understand one another. If our environments differ, we may misunderstand each other. Here is an example of how differing personal
   environments can cause a misunderstanding. You're examining bro-
   chures for colleges you wish to attend, and you're somewhat frustrated because you can't figure out how you and your parents, who
   are financially burdened, are going to pay for any of these schools.
   Your friend wanders up, asks you what the problem is, and when
   you say you are upset and worried about how to pay for college, she
   says, "Write a check, like my dad did!" She believes she is helping to
   solve your problem. You believe she is being uncaring, and you're
   irritated with her for not being more sensitive regarding your financial situation. The real problem is that her personal environment, or
   experience (she comes from a wealthy family), is not the same as

yours. She can't relate to your situation, and her message reflects this. The message she thought she sent wasn't the message received due to your different personal environments.

2. ***The sender did not properly encode the message.*** When you do not clearly encode your message, the other person will not understand what you mean. There are many reasons why a message may not be clearly encoded. We might leave something out because it seems obvious. For example, the person I am speaking to has just arrived to take me to a meeting. He was to pick me up at 6:00 but it is now 6:30. If the first message I send is, "You are really unreliable," without referring to it being a half an hour past the time we agreed to depart, he may not understand what I am talking about. He may be confused because in his mind, he's picking me up just like he said, reliable as ever. Another frequent cause of an unclear message is failing to express verbally what we are feeling. We cannot always rely on nonverbal signals, like facial expressions, to convey the intended message. You may think a person is angry with you because he is frowning as he speaks, when in fact the frown may be due to a headache. Effective communication requires a complete and clear message to be formatted both verbally and nonverbally in the encoding process *before* it is sent.

3. ***The receiver was distracted by noise.*** The final cause of misunderstandings is **noise**. Noise is anything that works to distract a communicator from hearing or listening. The stars on the model represent noise. There are two types of noise interference: external noise and internal noise. **External noise** is produced outside your body in the atmosphere surrounding you: machinery in operation, telephones ringing, children arguing, televisions blaring or other people talking are all examples of noise. External noise can also include distractions you don't hear, such as a hot room, smoke in the air, or an uncomfortable chair. External noise hinders our ability to hear or listen to what is said because we become distracted by the interference. This may cause us to lose all or part of the message being sent. We are also distracted by things happening inside our bodies. **Internal noise** consists of thoughts or feelings that we experience in our own minds and bodies. There are two types of internal noise. Internal psychological noise is that which occurs when you are preoccupied, daydreaming, or worrying about an exam, and therefore your thoughts distract you from listening to what is being said. Internal physical noise refers to distractions caused from your bodily functions, such as when you are hungry and your stomach is growling, or you are thirsty and your throat is dry. A person who is hearing impaired because of an accident or a bad cold will find it difficult to understand a verbal mes-

sage. Any, all, or a combination of these "noises" may result in not receiving the message sent.

Being aware of the process of communication and knowing where possible problems might occur in our communication are keys that will help you become a more effective communicator. Because let's face it, we all need to communicate!

Conclusion

Communication is a complex and dynamic process. It is an essential ingredient for survival in our world. Better understanding of how the communication process works and its importance in your daily activities will help you make a commitment to the journey you have begun in your communication course. The quality, success, and fulfillment of your needs, wants, and desires are directly dependent on your ability to communicate effectively with those around you. Think about Jason and Susan. Effective communication could have helped them to eliminate their misunderstanding of each other's messages. Who knows, Susan might have been on that train with Jason, ready to celebrate!

DISCUSSION QUESTIONS

1. Do you agree with the authors that communication is the key to survival? List several reasons to support your opinion.

2. Describe and illustrate the communication process using a "real-life" example.

3. Name three reasons a receiver may misinterpret your message. Use a specific example of a time the message you sent was misinterpreted; discuss why you think the message went astray.

4. How can our intrapersonal communication be noise?

5. Explain how it might be helpful to the communication process if two people who shared similar personal environments were communicating with one another.

KEY TERMS

axioms	intrapersonal communication
channel	mass communication
communication	message
decoding	noise
encoding	personal environment
external noise	public communication
feedback	small group communication
internal noise	society
interpersonal communication	symbols

chapter two

Verbal Communication

Say What?

CHAPTER HIGHLIGHTS

- Language is a system of words that is rule guided.
- These words are symbols, and we use them to create messages that have common meaning to other people.
- When we speak or write words, we are using verbal communication.
- Language is used for labeling, defining, limiting, clarifying, evaluating, and verifying.
- Language requires a conscious effort that uses a singular process.
- Language can be arbitrary and troublesome.
- Misuse of language includes the use of jargon, euphemisms, and inflated language.
- Verbal communication can be more effective if we reduce confusion and ambiguity by anticipating before we speak and asking for clarification from others.

Would this train never get to his station, thought Jason? All he wanted to do was get home. All the talking going on around him was annoying him, and he was already mad. Why hadn't Susan met him at the train station like he had asked her to? He clearly remembered telling her to meet him at the station and not to be late—that it was important. She couldn't have misunderstood what he said. It wasn't like he was talking in a foreign language. He replayed the day's phone conversation over again in his head. He was absolutely sure he had said, "Susan, meet me at the station at 5:00. Please don't be late; it is really important to me." Jason prided himself on having good communication skills. He knew it was important to be clear and precise. His message had been just that; no, she couldn't have misunderstood. That meant she had deliberately stood him up. Three years together and she had stood him up! As Jason mentally urged the train to go faster, two words echoed in his head. They were "the station" over and over again.

"No, I haven't had time to see that display at the museum," Susan answered the cabbie. Just her luck to get a chatty cab driver! Susan wanted him to shut up. In fact she just wanted everyone to be quiet. People had been talking to her all day, sometimes two at a time, like when Jason called and her assistant had been asking another question. Most of all she wanted her own thoughts to be silent. She was tired and worried. Did Jason really want to break up with her after three years? Why hadn't she had some clue this was happening? She'd actually thought he might be ready to take their relationship to a new level, and now he'd

stood her up. She replayed this morning's conversation in her head, "Susan, meet me at The Station at 5:00. Please don't be late; it is really important to me." She knew that's what he had said. She couldn't possibly have misunderstood. She knew she had been late and he had specifically asked her not to be, but she was only fifteen minutes late and she had called to tell him that. If it was important to him, why hadn't he waited? Susan had such wonderful memories about the times they had spent at The Station; it was their place, where they had met. Obviously she wasn't confused as to where The Station was located. "Lady, I gotta pick up a fare at the train station that is going to the same area as you. Since we pass by the station would you mind if I pick this person up and you share the fare?' asked the cabbie. Susan's confused mind snapped back to the driver. The station, Susan thought—the train station? Had Jason meant for her to meet him at the train station?

What Is Verbal Communication?

Now that we have discussed the process of communication by examining the communication model, we can continue our exploration of interpersonal communication. As we learned from the model, we encode and send messages to others. This is done in two different ways: verbally (with language) and nonverbally (anything that is not language). In this chapter we will take a closer look at **verbal communication**.

It is estimated that we spend nearly two-thirds of our day or more engaged in verbal communication. We talk to our peers, receive instructions at work, answer the phone, send e-mail, and tell our children when to be home for dinner. All of these tasks involve verbal communication. We use **language**, a complex system of symbols (words) that is rule guided, to create messages that have common meaning to other people. We use language so much in our daily lives that we often take it for granted. Think of how many times you use words to accomplish some daily task. Chances are you couldn't get through a single day without words. You might give verbal directions to your children in the morning by telling them to eat their breakfast, or write yourself a note to pick up bread on the way home from work. You jump into your car, place the gearshift in drive, turn on the lights, and if it is raining, turn on the wipers. These simple tasks that relate to driving a car utilize words or symbols. As you drive, you stop at a stop sign, another use of words. If you stop to get donuts, you speak to the clerk to give your order. We could continue with these examples through your daily routine, but we really don't think it is necessary. You can begin to understand the important role that words, or language, has in our lives. Let's face it, language, whether spoken or written, is a necessary and powerful tool. Unfortunately, it is often taken for granted, and frequently used in such a way that misunderstandings result. Making sense about what someone says is difficult because of the complex nature of language and its many rules.

Uses of Language

Now that you have a little better idea what language is, we need to consider the many ways we use language. As we discuss how we commonly use language, keep in mind that we use it in both its written and spoken forms. More simply stated, we can write words or we can speak words. For the following we will refer primarily to communication done through the spoken word, but much will apply to our written communication as well.

- **We *use language to label or define.*** One of the primary ways we use language is to express our thoughts and feelings. Since we can't read each others' minds, we need to have a way of converting our mental images and emotions into some symbol that others can understand, as we learned in chapter 1. During this encoding process we pick and choose symbols we believe will be interpreted by others in the same manner that we interpret them. We also use this process to help us describe objects, people, and experiences to others. This use of words or language helps us to label or define our thoughts clearly, so that others may understand and interpret those very same ideas.

- **We *use language to limit and clarify.*** When we speak, we often use words like *most, some, all, none, every, few, one, many,* etc. This is a means by which we can limit or be more specific in our messages to others. By clarifying our message with words that quantify, we can eliminate misunderstandings that can occur because of too many word interpretations. For example, when I say, "I want ALL of the cookies," you have a pretty good idea that I want more than one or two. This quantifying word, all, helps you to limit or eliminate all other possible interpretations to my message, thereby clarifying my intention.

- **We *use language to evaluate.*** Language also allows us to share our perceptions with others. Are you stingy or frugal? Is something adequate or average? Is the course worthwhile or a waste of time? Is someone wicked or compassionate? The words we choose in an attempt to evaluate someone or something can convey to another person our values or judgment of some entity. These evaluations and perceptions will differ from person to person, but language allows us to form and share our opinions and experiences with others.

- *We use language to verify.* One of the most effective uses of language is for message verification. We can verify that the messages we send are actually the messages received. We can request feedback in order to limit communication breakdowns. We can use language to discuss language by asking, "Do you understand what I mean," or "Did I explain that sufficiently?"

Language serves many purposes in our daily lives. Language allows us to talk about things that are outside our immediate experience. We can talk about the past and the future. We can share hopes, goals, and dreams, or share memories of last Christmas with our families. It helps us notice things, creates opportunities, facilitates coordination of our social lives, and shapes our identities. For these reasons it is a powerful tool. Just like any tool it needs to be correctly and safely used. Because language is so prevalent we sometimes forget to use this tool wisely. In order to make our verbal communication more effective, we need to understand the characteristics of language and where language can become troublesome.

Characteristics of Language

Language is intended to improve understanding between and among people. However, our verbal communication often results in misunderstandings due to its complex nature. Let's take a closer look at some predominant characteristics of language to see if we can better understand how miscommunication can result.

- *Language is conscious.* Language is our *primary* form of communication. This does not mean it is the most powerful form of communication, but it means that when we use it, we are consciously making an effort to do so. While we sometimes say that we speak before we think, this is not really so. In chapter 1 we learned that we initially think in pictures and must go through the encoding process to form an actual message. During this process, we most often choose language as the means to convey our message. We make a conscious effort, or choice, to do so.

Think about it. We can send a message quickly by speaking words. We can say hello, tell someone to turn right, or place an order from a catalog, all in a few short seconds. We quickly jot down a note, and leave it for someone to read later. With language, we don't necessarily have to be *with* a person to communicate with him. We can send an e-mail, post a question on a bulletin board, or chat online on the computer. Try to imagine a single day without language. What would you do if you suddenly had no words to convey your thoughts and feelings to others? Would you mime, or carry around a box full of pictures that could be used like flash cards when you wanted to communicate? A day without language would be cumbersome and inconvenient. Language is a convenient, time-saving tool, one that we make a conscious effort to use.

- *Language is a singular process.* As the previous examples show, we can send a message by either speaking or writing words. The process of using language is singular; words are a single element used to convey an idea to someone else. This concept makes language discrete, meaning when we choose to use it our message is encoded with a clear beginning and end. The message has distinct and separate elements, the words themselves. This is not the case with nonverbal communication—a process composed of several elements, such as gesturing, facial expressions, or posture. All of these elements can occur simultaneously to convey a message, as we will discover in the next chapter.

- *Language is arbitrary.* Wait, you say, language isn't random and arbitrary. Words have specific and precise meanings. We have dictionaries that lend proof to this fact. All we really have to do, if we don't know the meaning of a word, is look the word up in the dictionary. We are then provided with that word's precise meaning. Well, that sounds logical, but let's look closer at this assumption.

All words have two different kinds of meanings. They have denotative and connotative meanings. **Denotative** meanings are those dictionary definitions referred to previously. If you look a word up in a dictionary or online, you'll find how the word is most commonly being used. That's how dictionaries are written. Careful research is done to discover how people are using words and that's what is recorded in the dictionary. The most common usage of the word will be listed first, but you may find more than one definition of the word. These multiple definitions may be very diverse in meaning. For example the word *gay* will contain definitions that include both "happily excited" and "homosexual" (*Merriam-Webster's 11th Collegiate Dictionary*, 2003). Both denotative meanings for this word are in the dictionary, but depending on why you are using the word, very different messages are sent or received.

Let's assume for a moment that we share the same denotative meaning of a word with someone else. Will our language or use of this word still be random and arbitrary? The answer may be yes because words also have connotative meanings.

Connotative meanings describe the feelings and experiences connected to words by individuals. Consider the word *snow*. Most people will have a very similar idea of a denotative meaning for that word. It will be something like "frozen precipitation in the form of flakes." Yet the connotative meaning each person has of the word *snow* can be very different depending upon his or her own personal environment, as discussed in chapter 1. For example, most skiers have happy experiences related to previous outings on the snow slopes. When they hear the forecast is for snow, they are excited and anticipate another enjoyable day of skiing. Now, let's take a skier but change her experience. Last year this skier had a bad accident; she broke a leg, had multiple bruises and lacerations, suffered a concussion, and spent a week in the hospital. Instead of enjoying the week's vacation as planned (and the deposits on accommodations weren't refundable!), our skier spent her vacation in pain and misery. Understandably, *this* skier might be reluctant to hit the slopes again. Snow might mean something completely different to that person than the first skier. What do you think *snow* means to an 85-year-old woman with osteoporosis and a hip replacement? Again, the connotative meaning would be associated with feelings and experiences very different from a 10-year-old who is glad to have a day off from school! Far from anticipating a day of sledding and having fun with friends, our elderly woman may view snow as meaning she will be completely homebound, isolated and controlled by the weather. Our connotative meanings for words are just as much a part of what the word means to us as are the denotative meanings in dictionaries.

Due to the possibility that people can use different denotative meanings of a word—and are as many connotative meanings as there are people—we can say that words themselves don't have meanings, rather people do. Words are only symbols. These symbols represent our ideas. Symbols are not always used in the same way by all people. Even in our common everyday language, we use the same word numerous ways. When we use a word to convey an idea, we need to understand that those receiving our message may base the meaning of a word on their own unique perception and experience. Words can be used by anyone to mean anything. It is only the commonality of the meaning of those words (both denotatively and connotatively) that gives us the ability to effectively communicate. This is why personal environments must "overlap" if a message is to be interpreted the way the sender intended. All too often we fail to understand how random or arbitrary our words may seem to others. This lack of understanding can lead to serious communication trouble.

Our Misuse of Language

Language, as we have learned, can be used to clarify our thoughts and define our feelings, among other uses. Since verbal communication is a conscious behavior we actually have the opportunity to avoid confusion with our language by choosing words that have common meanings. However, we don't always do this, whether it be consciously or unconsciously. In order to choose the most appropriate words for our messages we need to understand how certain uses of language can distort the messages we send. We also need to be aware that some people confuse others through the use of certain words. Typically groups of people (families, coworkers, and friends) develop their own languages. Such sublanguages are variations of our more commonly used language. While these sublanguages serve the group well, they can be confusing to those outside the group. We will discuss three types of language that can cause problems in communication: jargon, euphemisms, and inflated language. Let's define and explore these troublesome language areas.

Jargon

One misuse of language is called jargon. **Jargon** is developed and utilized within groups for use by that group. It often occurs in industry-specific situations. In other words, institutions create an entire language for use within their own area of expertise. Take for instance the medical field. If you are in a hospital, you might hear the words "stat" or "code blue." These are jargon words used by hospital personnel to indicate a very serious situation. A doctor might tell a nurse to medicate a patient QID. This is medical jargon for four times daily. Jargon is okay as long as everyone is in agreement about what the words mean. If everyone in the room is a hospital or health worker, then medical jargon is appropriate. If they are computer technicians, they might be confused by these words, resulting in ineffective communication.

Computer technicians use "RAM," "ROM," "byte" and "bit." People in the business world use "ASAP" and "PDQ" to indicate that a project must be done in a timely manner. With the popularity of chat rooms on the Internet, a whole new world of jargon has emerged. Laughing out loud (LOL), be back later (BBL), and rolling on the floor laughing (ROFL) are online jargon. This use of words within the appropriate group is quite effective, but if we carry this language into our daily communications, we can cause misunderstandings and problems among people outside the group.

Euphemisms

The second type of confusing language used by groups is known as euphemisms. A **euphemism** is a word substituted for another word that we find too graphic, unpleasant, or painful to use. For instance, instead of saying someone has died, we say he "expired," or "passed away," or "went to heaven." Euphemisms are a convenient way to buffer a message that might be distressing or upsetting. Euphemisms are acceptable and effective as long as everyone agrees on the substitution, but this isn't always the case. When someone uses a word to represent a particular type of situation and other people know what the person is talking about, everything is fine. However, when a person uses a euphemism he has created or one that is not commonly known or agreed upon, that same word may confuse everyone else.

For example, the government is notorious for abusing words through their use of euphemisms. They have created an entire network of "substitutes" for many unpleasant scenarios. The problem is they have not shared this with the rest of us! Take for example, spent fuel (toxic waste), neutralize (kill), or a peace mission (sending troops to fight). This use of language is unacceptable. In these instances, the choice of substitute words is misleading and does not make a situation less painful or offensive. If anything, we are more confused when we figure out the real intent behind words of this type. Another perhaps more humorous example that many of you will remember is the term "wardrobe malfunction" as it was used to signify Janet Jackson's exposed breast during the 2004 half-time performance at the Super Bowl. Saying it was a wardrobe malfunction is more neutral and less offensive, especially when used with people who think public nudity is outrageous and immoral, than saying exactly what happened. Euphemisms are only acceptable uses of language if we can collectively and consistently agree on their appropriateness as substitute words.

Inflated Language

Language that accentuates by making something seem better, larger, nicer, more desirable, less common, or more important is called **inflated language**. Advertisers are especially fond of inflated language. They often avoid negative consumer impressions by inflating product language. They will use words like home-style, plus-size, and domestic to paint a more favorable picture of their product or service. Simulated leather, leather look-alike, near leather, and pleather are all inflated language for vinyl.

Mary's husband is an avid golfer. He and his fellow golfing buddies visit many courses over the spring and summer. They like to try out new courses and particularly enjoy difficult play. Unfortunately, the harder the course, the more strokes one uses. One of the golfers says that these additional strokes make the ball "experienced." He believes that an experienced golf ball is a better golf ball. The rest of the golfers find this attitude amusing. The golf ball is used or misused (a lot) depending on your perception; it is not experienced. This is a perfect example of the concept of inflated language. Inflated language attempts to "puff" something up like an inflated beach ball. This often makes an item sound better than it really is!

Human resource departments at companies have begun to use inflated language as a cheap means of boosting employee morale. It seems much more important to be called an access technician than a doorman.

Activity for Further Understanding

Identifying Language Misuse

This exercise will help you to see how often we use the three categories of troublesome language that we have described above. You are to find ten common examples of

1. Jargon
2. Euphemisms
3. Inflated Language.

Look in magazines, TV ads, newspapers, pop-up ads, or listen to other people conversing. Bring your examples to the next class. All members of the class should compare their examples. Are there duplicates? Are the examples words that you commonly use? Are some of the words used by you and your classmates on a daily basis? Do these words cause confusion? How can we eliminate these troublesome words from our routine vocabulary?

Here are some more; price integrity coordinator (checker), communication controller (switchboard operator), automotive diagnostician (repairman), and petroleum transfer engineer (gas station attendant).

The problem with inflated language is that it creates an impression of a situation that is more favorable than its reality. It "sounds" better and may lead the person hearing this type of language to misinterpret the real intent of the words. If we are striving for mutual understanding, we must choose *accurate* words to depict a situation. We shouldn't attempt to mislead or confuse people. If we are selling used cars, we should say, "used cars." If an item is not leather, say it is vinyl. We can avoid trouble by calling a rose a *rose*.

Suggestions for Effective Verbal Communication

Since the only message that really matters is the one that is received (whether or not that was the one you intended to send) it is time to turn our attention to ways in which we can improve our verbal communication. Having our messages received incorrectly is frustrating for all parties involved. Under some circumstances it can also be dangerous. Remembering the uses and abuses of language that we have already considered can help you make more appropriate choices about your own language. We also suggest the following guidelines for reducing confusion and ambiguous language that results in misunderstandings.

Reduce Confusion and Ambiguity

While it is impossible to guarantee that a message, no matter how carefully constructed, will reach its audience in the way you intended, you can reduce the possibility of confusion.

- Use *specific words* that narrow options. Choose words that decrease ambiguity by identifying a particular group within a general category. For example, say, "Mary and Tracey both have cats" not "Mary and Tracey both have pets."

- Use *concrete words* that appeal to our senses. This helps your audience receive and decode messages by allowing them to conjure up a picture. Words that describe sounds, sights, smells, and feelings help us clarify abstract ideas. For example, say, "The evening sky combined magenta, pale blues, and golden tones of light" not "The evening sky was pretty." The first example creates a visual, sensory experience that is lacking in the second. It sends a clearer message.

- Use *precise words* to accurately express meaning. While most words have several denotative and innumerable connotative meanings, some words are still more precise than others. They provide meanings that help us arrive at a mutual interpretation. For example, words such as each, every, or all help us understand a precise quantity. When there isn't a more precise word, specify a detail (barely, minimally, etc.).

Anticipate Before You Speak

While a great deal of our day-to-day communication is impromptu (created for a specific situation without preparation) that doesn't mean we can't think about what we are saying. We're sure you have all been advised to "think before you speak" so you won't "put your foot in your mouth." How many of us wish we had heeded that excellent advice? We think much faster than we speak. Therefore we have a chance to think about what we want to say. For example, if someone isn't acting responsibly you could confront the person by saying, "You never do your share of the work," or you could say, "I had to do one of your chores yesterday." Both convey the same general message, but the second message is much less likely to produce a defensive reaction. It is more likely to keep the channel of communication open.

Like the previous suggestion, if you anticipate how your message may be interpreted before you speak, you can avoid misunderstandings. By keeping the characteristics, problems, and suggestions for improving your verbal communication in mind, you may be able to send clearer messages.

Ask for Clarification

Finally, when you are communicating with others, don't be afraid to "check" your own interpretation of what words mean. It is perfectly acceptable (and doesn't sound stupid) to say, "When you say _____, do you mean _____?" You should also request feedback from someone you are talking with if there appears to be a communication breakdown. Sometimes, by simply clarifying another person's use of a word, you can avoid an impending breakdown.

Conclusion

The use of language, or verbal communication, is one of our primary forms of communication. It is convenient, but it can be problematic also. Because language is arbitrary and words are symbols that can be interpreted in multiple ways, we often experience a breakdown in our communication with others. We must always be aware that just because we know what we mean we are not assured that our message will be perceived in the same way by our audience. Being aware of where "messages can go astray" will help us create more effective ways of communicating interpersonally. Awareness is the first step in change. It isn't possible to be 100 percent sure that your message will be understood as you meant it to be, but thinking before you speak and applying what we've discussed here will greatly reduce the likelihood of misinterpretation.

DISCUSSION QUESTIONS

1. What is verbal communication?
2. What is the difference between connotative and denotative meanings? How can these different meanings lead to communication confusion?
3. What is meant by the phrase, "Meanings are in people, not words"?
4. Why should you avoid the use of jargon, euphemisms, and inflated language?
5. What are some ways you can better assure that the message you sent is received properly?

KEY TERMS

connotative   jargon
denotative   language
euphemism   verbal communication
inflated language

chapter three

Nonverbal Communication

You Don't Say!

CHAPTER HIGHLIGHTS

- Nonverbal communication does not use words to convey meaning.
- Nonverbal communication conveys meaning through many channels, including our behavior and our body.
- Nonverbal cues or signals convey messages to others.
- These messages can help us to present our self to others, manage our environment, and manage our language.
- We use nonverbal communication to substitute, to complement, and to regulate.
- Nonverbal communication is unconscious, occurs through many channels, and is continuous.
- Nonverbal communication can be arbitrary and troublesome.
- Difficulties with nonverbal communication can be attributed to: cultural influence, first impressions, and gender.
- Nonverbal communication can be more effective if we are aware of it, don't make assumptions about it, and get verbal confirmation of our interpretations.

In the words of the song, As Time Goes By, *a sigh is just a sigh, right? Wrong! Susan had arrived home. She was hungry, tired, and angry. She was mad at Jason for not waiting and mad with herself for the horrible day she had experienced. She slammed the door shut. What was up with Jason? He had been very abrupt on the phone. Maybe she had gotten the meeting place wrong, but he had barely given her time to reply, let alone ask any questions. He had spoken very quickly and had lowered his voice to where she could hardly hear him. Then he said goodbye and hung up. What was his problem anyway? He was usually very distinct and courteous on the phone. Besides, he must have noticed how stressed she was. He usually was very understanding about how hectic her job was. Yep, something was wrong alright. She shook her head and frowned. What a mess!*

Jason was sure Susan had not wanted to meet him. She had been abrupt on the phone. From her tone, she had sounded like she really didn't want to talk at all, especially with him. She had barely replied before he had hung up the phone. In fact, now that he thought about it, her tone had had an edge, she was mad alright. But did that mean she was mad at him? Well, not necessarily. But then she had stood him up. They say actions speak louder than words. He was getting more confused by the minute. He could not wait for the train to stop so that he could find a phone and call Susan. He frowned and shook his head, now regretting that he'd left his cell phone at the office. Obviously the evening hadn't progressed the way he'd planned. Susan and he were supposed to be celebrating now, not angry with each other. He had to get this mess straightened out. He wanted to know why she was acting so mad at him!

What Is Nonverbal Communication?

In the last chapter we learned about verbal communication, or language. Nonverbal communication, quite simply, is everything else. It means, *not* language. This type of communication does not use words to convey meaning. Although some nonverbal communication is done with the voice (*how* you say what you say), no words are actually used.

Have you ever responded to a question or request with a sigh? Maybe you rolled your eyes when a friend did something silly. Perhaps you used your hands, or finger, to signal someone in traffic. Mary has a certain expression she uses when she is annoyed. Her children know to avoid her when she gives the "look." She doesn't have to use any words, they just know! In other words, nonverbal communication uses *many* elements to send a message, none of which are words! These elements can be perceived by others without any words being spoken. Nonverbal messages are very powerful. When they are used along with words, they dramatically impact and "shape" the words you choose to encode your message. They are cues or signals that convey meaning. They can and are used instead of words in many instances. These cues use the body to communicate messages.

Types of Nonverbal Cues

Nonverbal communication conveys meaning through many channels including those that involve our behavior and our bodies. Many of our behaviors serve as **nonverbal cues** or signals that convey meanings to others. Although there are numerous ways to convey nonverbal messages, we'll look at the cues that have the most impact on our daily communication. We've divided them into three categories for easier association: those that help us to present our self to others; those that help us to manage our environment; and those that accompany our language, such as the tone, volume, and pitch of our voice.

Self-Presentation Cues

It is likely that when you think about nonverbal communication you think about body language. We literally "speak" with our bodies. *Facial expressions*, *posture*, and *gestures* are body cues or signals that send messages to others. Therefore, all human behaviors are essentially forms of communication, or body language.

We use behaviors to communicate messages to others. We use our *face and eyes* to send signals to each other. If we are surprised we might raise an eyebrow; if we are scared, we might open our eyes very wide. If we think an idea is crazy, we roll our eyes and gesture with our finger to our temple. We might raise our index finger to signal someone to wait a moment. We shake hands, give a high five, clap, raise our hands to talk, and use many other body movements to communicate with others. In fact, we use our bodies so often to send signals, that we are all familiar with the term *body language*. We even communicate through our *posture*. A relaxed posture sends a very different message than a stiff one. In a classroom you might see some students sitting up straight and looking at the instructor, while others are hunched over their desks looking at the floor. These two groups of students are conveying very different messages. Posture can send a message about power, indicate how we feel about ourselves, or signal how we feel about a topic of conversation. Think of the difference between a dog that has his ears perked up and his tail wagging and a dog whose ears are laid back and hangs his tail between his legs. The same types of postures are used by people. Even the way our bodies *look*, or our *physical body characteristics*, send a message.

We may not mean for our physique to convey a message, and we may not *like* the fact that people judge the way our bodies look, but it is true that our appearance sends a message. If we have uncombed hair or have not brushed our teeth, we send a message to others. If we have on wrinkled clothing or torn pants, we send a message. If we are overweight or underweight, we send a message. This seems unfair, but let's take a closer look. Remember, we said that as long as someone can see you, a message is sent whether you intended to send it or not. All human behavior is potential communication. Your physical characteristics are seen by others, and are often what people notice about you first. Others receive an impression of you based on your appearance and this becomes part of how they perceive you (perception is the subject of chapter 8). If you have uncombed hair and are overweight, you may not be taken as seriously as someone who is sporting the newest hairstyle and has an athletic build. This may seem ridiculous, but it is all based on the premise that appearance, or what people *see*, sends a message. That is why so much is determined from a person's "first impression" of you. Unfair maybe, but that *is* nonverbal communication at work.

Even your *clothing* sends a message. If you dress casually for a board meeting, your words may not be taken as seriously as the words of someone who is dressed in a three-piece suit. The importance of this form of nonverbal communication cannot be ignored. Clothing is a distinct form of nonverbal communication for many people. Think about teenagers and their choice of clothing. What is the difference between wearing designer blue jeans and no-name department store jeans? Our choices of jewelry, backpacks, and whether or not we have a tattoo sends a message. This form of nonverbal communication is a subcategory of clothing, known as **artifacts**. A Timex watch sends an entirely different message than a Rolex watch does. Earrings send a different message than nose rings, and hair clips send a different message than hair bows. Even though the message is based on someone else's interpretation, a *message* has still been communicated.

Another way we send nonverbal messages is through the use of *touch*. Essentially the United States is a noncontact culture. This means, in public, we mainly use touch for social rituals (like handshaking). Since touching another person facilitates intimate interaction, it can be a powerful form of nonverbal communication that makes forceful statements about relationships. For example, we assume two people holding hands care about each other, while a fistfight implies the opposite interpretation.

As you can see, we use our body in a variety of ways to send messages to others. Whether or not we intend to send those messages, our nonverbal cues serve as a way that we present ourselves to others. These cues also help us convey messages to others about how we relate to our external environment.

Environmental Management Cues

Less obvious to most of us is how our body language sends a message about how we relate to our external environment. For example, we exist and move our bodies through space and time. How much time you spend working on something or communicating with a person sends a message. The activities you engage in during your time send a message (do you spend more time working or more time with your family?). And we mustn't forget to mention that how punctual or late you are for events sends a message to others.

Proxemics, how we use or move through space, communicates a message to others. The distance or proximity around and between us and other people sends a definite message. Researchers tell us that there are four spaces to consider when observing proximity as a form of nonverbal communication. They are intimate, personal, social, and public space.

Intimate space is the closest of the four distances. In fact, intimate space is so close it is hardly a distance at all. Touching and other forms of physical contact are included in intimate space. If we had to put a measurement on this distance, most researchers would say it starts with skin contact and moves up to about 12 inches. Most people reserve this area for people with whom they are extremely comfortable.

Personal space is about an arm's length from your body in both directions. Stand up a moment and extend your arms to the side. Now rotate your body one full turn around. This invisible circle is your personal space. If we place a measurement on this distance, it would extend approximately twelve to thirty-six inches. You may not like anyone to invade "your space" or cross into this invisible "bubble." Yet others are comfortable letting people into their bubble. Some may even be comfortable letting people into their intimate space. However, most people reserve these two spaces for close friends, family members, or their intimate partners. Whether or not you allow others into these spaces depends on many factors including past experiences, cultural social influences, and gender.

The third type of space is known as **social space**. This is the area or distance that we reserve for social interactions or social occasions. Think of being at a party or a picnic where there are many people present. How close can you be to these people without feeling uncomfortable? Many textbooks suggest a distance of four to fifteen feet as the measurement for social space. We, your authors, believe that this is arbitrary. We can define social space as that distance that occurs in a social situation. The actual measurement of this area will depend on the individual and her personal comfort level as well as the type of social situation occurring.

The fourth and final distance is that of **public space**. This is the distance we encounter in public situations. These may include classrooms, train stations, bus terminals, airplanes, theaters, or concert halls. Many communication researchers suggest fifteen feet or more as the proper distance for public space. It is difficult to say exactly what distance constitutes this area. Most of our public areas in society today invade not only our personal space, but often our intimate space as well. Think of the last time you were at the theater and had to share an armrest and drink holder with the stranger next to you. Have you flown anywhere lately? What do you think of the "public space" afforded to you on the plane? Since public spaces usually involve strangers, most people prefer greater distances in these areas, and will often seek to put as much distance as possible between themselves and others. When we walk into our dentist's waiting room, we typically don't choose to sit next to others. We choose a seat away from other people we don't know. We define our public space.

Regardless of the distances or precise measurements in any of these four spaces, a message is communicated by how we utilize, move about in, or avoid these spaces. Your body movement and how close you are to others, your proximity, communicates a distinct message about your comfort level with those around you. Distance is powerful in interpersonal communication, so powerful that we often assume ownership of the space around us. This concept is known as **territoriality**. Have you ever been in a classroom and avoided sitting in the corner chair, because a certain student *always* sits *there?* Since everyone knows this, you all sit elsewhere. This is territoriality. That particular student seems to own that particular space (the chair in the corner). I (Mary) used to share a room with my sister. She had one half, and I had the other. My mother did not paint a line down the center of the room, but we both knew where it was! If one of us crossed into the other one's territory there was trouble. We had assumed ownership of this space and did not want the other sister to violate it.

Space is a powerful communication tool. Think of a boss who has you sit ten feet away from his desk when discussing a problem, versus the boss who asks you to pull up a chair and talk. What message is sent when a bank ropes off where you can stand and where you can't? All of these uses of space communicate messages of ownership, or territorial rights. We borrow this concept from animals. Many animals behave in various ways to "mark" their territory. While we may not use the same methods (thank goodness), the end result is the same: our yard is marked by a fence; our parking space is marked by a sign.

Our use and "ownership" of space aren't the only nonverbal cues related to the environment. Even temperature, lighting, and use of color communicate a message. For example, the temperature of a room can inhibit or stimulate communication, alter our mood, or affect our attention span.

Lighting affects our moods. Bright lights encourage activity and boisterous conversation while soft lighting soothes and calms, encouraging more serious conversation. Think about the difference in lighting in a fast-food restaurant versus a quality restaurant. The fact that it is brighter in one and softer in the other sends a different message. The bright lights in the fast-food restaurant say, "eat and move on." The softer lighting in the more expensive restaurant says, "enjoy, linger, and dine."

Our use of color also sends a nonverbal message. The color of our clothes and the paint color we use to decorate our walls all send messages. Research shows that people react both emotionally and physically to color. Red excites and stimulates, while blue comforts and soothes. Yellow is cheery and has been found to elevate our moods, whereas pink has a negative effect upon physical strength. We often choose color as a way to communicate to others. It becomes a cue for how we have attempted to manage our external environment.

So how we manage our external environment sends a nonverbal message like our body language does. Nonverbal literally means "no words" and the environment around us and our bodies certainly don't imply the use of actual words. What about a third category of nonverbal cues that affects words but is not words? These elements accompany language and occur when we use our voice.

Language Management Cues

Before reading any further take yourself back to your childhood. Think about a time you asked one of your parents if you could do something and his or her reply was, "maybe." Now, the denotative meaning of maybe is 50 percent yes and 50 percent no, but we bet you knew from the *way* your parent said the word whether you were or weren't going to get to do what you asked. The nonverbal message implied by the tone, inflection, or volume of your parent's voice gave you your answer. These elements are known as **paralanguage**.

There are nonverbal communications made by the *voice* that are not words or language. There are characteristics of the voice and many ways we use the voice that can communicate a message. We can vary our pitch, tone, or volume, depending on the message we wish to communicate. If we are angry, we may raise our voice and use a sarcastic tone. Mothers often use a language called "motherese" to speak to infants. This language is based on a series of varying pitches used with or without words. These variations and fluctuations in our vocal quality send a definite message to others. Sometimes, we use sounds instead of words as communication. We might mumble ugh, huh, or mmm. A similar type of nonword, such as ah or oh, might be used for emphasis. Unfortunately, the use of the voice is very *ambiguous*. It is difficult to determine *what* the communicator is trying to communicate when paralanguage is used. In fact, all forms of nonverbal communication can be confusing because the *receiver* of the message, *not* the sender, makes the determination about what a nonverbal signal means. The message intended frequently is not the message received because these determinations are based on many factors.

We even "read messages into" pitch (how high or low a tone is), volume (how loud or soft), rate (how quickly or slowly we speak), and quality (resonance) of the tone. A higher pitched tone may be "read" to indicate fear, surprise, or femininity. Someone who increases his or her volume and speaks loudly may be thought of as domineering and commanding attention, where a soft-spoken person may be considered weak. The rate or speed in which we deliver a message can indicate excitement, and the quality of the voice (raspy or nasal) may serve to annoy.

Although words are powerful, and we use them on a daily basis, from the above examples we can see that "body" words are also powerful. Nonverbal communication or cues are so powerful that they can affect and even modify the meaning of our spoken words.

Through the use of nonverbal cues we can change the meaning of our verbal communication. We can substitute, complement, and regulate the actual words we speak. In fact, those are the uses of nonverbal communication that we will explore next.

Uses of Nonverbal Communication

There are many ways to use nonverbal communication. Since we use nonverbal communication as an accompaniment to language (whether done intentionally or not) we need to be aware of how these uses impact our communication overall.

Sometimes our nonverbal cues *substitute* for language. We might wave instead of saying hello. We might point instead of saying "Turn right." We can use many signals, with the hands, body, or face, *instead* of using words. This is using nonverbal communication as a substitute for verbal communication. Used in this way, these nonverbal cues are a form of gesturing called **emblems**.

Sometimes we choose to speak, and then *complement* our words by adding a gesture. We say, "Turn right," and then point to the right. In these cases, we are not signaling as a substitution, but adding the signal to help clarify or emphasize our spoken words to someone else. These types of gestures are known as **illustrators** and they add to the verbal message we are sending.

Another way that we use nonverbal communication is to *regulate* our words. Regulating controls a verbal message by reinforcing it with a nonverbal signal. When a teacher asks you to be quiet, and then puts her finger to her mouth, she is regulating language. When a mother says no to a demanding toddler while she scrunches up her brow and points and wags her finger, she is regulating her words. When we use these cues to

Activity for Further Understanding

Nonverbal Rules

Now that you have learned that we can communicate without words, you are to put your knowledge to use. You are to create a handbook that lists rules for communicating without words. Your handbook must include a definition for each type of nonverbal communication that we have studied in this chapter, and three rules for communicating using those categories. Pretend that you are writing this handbook for someone who has never heard of nonverbal communication. How would you define communicating with the face and eyes? What "rules" do we follow in society for this form of communication? The following list will help you.

face/eyes	artifacts	lighting
gestures	physical body	voice tone
posture	clothing	voice rate
proxemics	touch	voice pitch
territoriality	temperature	

indicate an emotional response, like pounding on the table and saying, "I'm right!" they are called **affect displays**. These add power and reinforce the meaning of the words we speak.

Characteristics of Nonverbal Communication

Nonverbal communication is complex because there are so many different types of nonverbal cues. We don't always realize it when we communicate nonverbally. If we are familiar with the characteristics of nonverbal communication we can have a better understanding of how to avoid the communication problems and misunderstandings that are often caused by nonverbal communication. Nonverbal communication has several characteristics: it occurs unconsciously; it occurs through many channels; it can be continuous; and it is arbitrary. Let's look at these characteristics.

Nonverbal Communication Is Unconscious

Nonverbal communication is, for the most part, unconscious. Our nonverbal cues often are a result of our intrapersonal communication. This internal communication causes us to form expressions on our face, move our body a certain way, or raise the volume of our voice as a reaction to our internal thoughts and feelings. This often happens without our awareness. In other words, our physical reactions are unconscious. They are rarely planned by us. Our bodies automatically react to our thoughts. This causes an interesting situation as far as communication is concerned. These unconscious actions become *body language* and can be viewed by other people. People will make a determination about our behavior based on *their* internal thoughts and perceptions. Nonverbal messages frequently are misinterpreted. Say you are thinking about the history test that you have tomorrow. Without being aware of it, you frown. I see the frown and think you are mad. Your nonverbal, unconscious frown was interpreted by me as anger (a message you weren't even aware you were sending), not worry. All behavior can be potential communication. If someone sees you, your behavior sends a message. It doesn't matter whether you intended to communicate or not; it happened. Although nonverbal communication is unconscious, it is very powerful. Often the impact or meaning of our message *comes* from our nonverbals, even if we use language at the same time.

Nonverbal Communication Occurs through Many Channels

Nonverbal cues come in many forms and often involve multiple channels. For example, if something startles us we might grimace, throw our arms up, and scream all at the same time. Thus, our facial expression and the movement of our arms and our scream signal our surprise or even fear as a result of being startled. We are bombarded with nonverbal messages because there are so many channels through which they can be sent. There are so many that it is difficult to interpret all of them. Furthermore, we often use nonverbal cues, such as paralanguage, simultaneously with verbal communication to give additional meaning to the words we speak.

Nonverbal Communication Is Continuous

While verbal communication is discrete, nonverbal communication is continuous. At any given time, whether or not we mean to, we are continually sending and receiving numerous nonverbal messages. In fact, such nonverbal cues are so abundant and nonending that we can say it is impossible to NOT communicate nonverbally. Even when we are asleep we are communicating nonverbally! You may be curled up on the couch taking a nap, not even aware that another person is in the room. Are you sending a message to that person? Of course you are. The message is that you are sleeping. It's not a message you thought about or even intended to send but nevertheless it is communicated. All human behavior is potential communication as long as it is observed by another person. If you consider the fact that we send and receive such cues on an ongoing basis, you can see why nonverbal messages might be missed or misunderstood.

Nonverbal Communication Is Often Arbitrary

Like our use of verbal communication, our use of nonverbal communication can often be random or arbitrary, but for very different reasons. Remember, nonverbal cues are often unconscious behaviors. We may gesture or make an inflection without actually giving it much thought, and we might not consciously attach any real meaning to this behavior. Nevertheless, a person who is watching us might attach meaning to the behavior. Crossing your arms may be simply a comfortable position for you that you assume randomly when you are listening to someone else speak. Yet, to the speaker, your crossed arms may indicate that you are irritated or are opposed to what she is saying. Maybe you have a headache that is causing you to scowl, but to others you appear angry. Your vocal inflections, your gestures, or your facial expressions may mean something different to you than to the listener or observer. The fact that nonverbal cues are arbitrary can be troublesome and cause communication to be difficult.

Nonverbal communication can be very confusing. We have learned that much of our nonverbal communication is done unconsciously. More importantly, we have learned that the receiver of the message, not the sender, determines its meaning. Since many nonverbal cues are formed with the body, they appear differently due to our unique nature as human beings. Additionally, our interpretation or determination of nonverbal signals will be influenced by our own individual experiences.

Difficulties with Nonverbal Communication

Our individual experiences are comprised of many elements that influence how we use and interpret nonverbal cues. We will discuss three influences—culture, first impressions, and gender—which increase the difficulty of understanding nonverbal communication.

Culture

Each communication experience is different because we are unique individuals. Our experiences are molded by our culture. Most nonverbal cues are dependent upon the culture or society in which they are used. In fact there are only six facial expressions that are used universally to represent various emotions. In most cultures, facial expressions that represent anger, fear, disgust, surprise, sadness, and happiness are similar, but circumstances that are acceptable for displaying these expressions are not the same across cultures. Gestures vary a great deal from country to country as well. In fact, a circle made by connecting the thumb to the forefinger of the same hand is a sign for the sex act in some cultures, but in the United States it means everything is okay. The use of space or proxemics is also culture specific. South Americans typically stand closer to one another than North Americans or Australians. Other nonverbal cues may result in different cultural interpretations as well. Acceptable clothing styles, touch, and physical body characteristics can differ depending upon what region or country a person is from. Nonverbal cues are influenced by culture.

First Impressions

You have probably heard that first impressions are lasting impressions. This is true. Just as we may not like the fact that people perceive us by how we dress or comb our hair, we may think it ridiculous that how someone perceived us when we were first introduced would help or hinder our future interactions with her. After all, how we appeared at that time isn't necessarily indicative of how we usually are; we aren't always a fashion plate or on our best behavior. Unfortunately that doesn't matter. Numerous studies have concluded that the first thoughts and feelings connected to a person we have just met form a fundamental and lasting impression of that person. These impressions tend to influence any further interactions. For example, consider meeting someone on a blind date. How quickly will you form opinions about the person and the evening ahead of you? Will it take you five minutes, an hour, or do you wait until the date comes to an end? The answer is you form an opinion in about 30 seconds! What about a job interview? How much time do you have to make a favorable impression on a potential employer? You may think that the interviewer's impressions are formed over the entire course of the interview, and a decision will be made afterward on hiring you. However, the decision is actually made in the first two minutes of your interview. In situations like these, not only are first impressions vitally important, you probably won't get a second chance to change negative impressions. Even more troubling is that men and women use nonverbal cues completely differently, causing varying first impressions and further misunderstandings.

Gender

Men and women so often cross-communicate that we will devote an entire chapter (7) to gender communication. For now, we will focus on the different way the sexes use nonverbal cues and how they are frequently misinterpreted.

In the United States, women tend to have more frequent eye contact during conversations and hold that contact longer than men regardless of whom they are communicating with. Because men use eye contact differently, they often misinterpret prolonged eye contact by women as an indicator of personal interest when in fact that may not be the case. Men's and women's facial expressions often convey very different meanings as well. When men smile, it is almost always a sign that they are pleased and exhibiting a positive reaction. Women smile more often, yet their smiles are harder to interpret. Female smiles generally relate to friendliness and affiliation, but are also used to hide other emotions that they don't want people to see.

Gestures are also used differently by the sexes. Women tend to keep their arms close to their bodies; men use their arms to expand their space and territory. Men often view confined gesturing as a sign of being timid or passive, while women see men's more expansive gesturing as rude and intrusive. Women tend to lean toward a person speaking and maintain eye contact. Men often lean away and let their eyes roam. This results in a woman thinking that the man she is speaking to isn't listening to her. Women tend to play with their hair or clothing more then men, which is often misinterpreted by men as a sign of nervousness or being uncomfortable. Men tap their fingers or hands on surfaces, resulting in women perceiving men as impatient and uninterested, which is often a misinterpretation.

The sexes have different touching behaviors as well. Research shows that, overall, women tend to touch others less than men, but value touch more. Women see touch as a sign of warmth and affection. Therefore they are more apt to touch other women rather than men. Women touch each other more frequently than men touch other men. For example, it is more common to see women walking arm in arm than it is to see men doing so. Women will dance with each other, whereas men rarely dance together. Men, according to research, touch others more frequently than women but for very different reasons. Typically men use touch to assert authority or to initiate sexual contact.

Men and women move through space differently. Men expand into space; they spread out their arms and legs in an attempt to signify power and gain territory. Women are less expansive even when they have power, and contract space when not in power. Both touching behavior and use of space can lead to numerous misunderstandings about power, control, and territory.

Suggestions for
Effective Nonverbal Communication

Now that we've reviewed the characteristics of nonverbal communication and the various elements that influence it, we can see how powerful it is in our daily communications. We need to interpret it carefully. Let's look at some practical suggestions for doing this. These will help us more effectively use and interpret nonverbal cues.

- *Be aware.* Pay attention to nonverbal cues, both the ones you send and those you receive. A lot is communicated through our body and voice. Much of our nonverbal communication is sent unconsciously, and as we've learned, our awareness of it is frequently low. Listen and look for nonverbal cues that are being sent. When something is said, notice the tone, pitch, rate, and volume of the voice (aside from the words spoken). What indicators are there that the person is asking a question, being funny or sarcastic? A quivering vocal tone might indicate nervousness or excitement. The words spoken might say one thing, but the tone of the voice might say something else. Facial expressions can also give clues to what is really being said. Are the words "I love this" accompanied by a smile or a frown? Remember that emotional messages are frequently not spoken but are implied through nonverbal communication. Ignoring nonverbal cues can leave you with an incomplete or misunderstood message. If you are attuned to nonverbal cues, you'll be better able to interpret the message.

- *Don't assume.* While you need to be aware of the nonverbal cues presented, you also need to make sure you don't assume you know what they mean. Your interpretation of those cues is just that, *your* interpretation. The sender may not have meant the message in that way. In fact, they may not have meant to send you a message at all! If you speak to someone and she frowns and doesn't reply, you may interpret her nonverbal communication to mean that she doesn't want to talk to you. In reality, the person may not even be aware that you have spoken to her because she is deep in thought about an unpleasant situation. Assuming that you *know* she doesn't want to talk to you would be a misinterpretation. It may seem safe to assume a person who is yelling and slamming doors is angry (based on his nonverbal language), but it wouldn't be safe to assume that *you* are the target of that anger, or that his anger is over something major. We need to remember that *our* interpretation may not match what the sender meant. In fact, making that kind of assumption often leads to misunderstandings.

• ***Get verbal confirmation.*** Whenever possible, get verbal confirmation of your interpretations. If you are the message sender, you can ask the other person what she thought about your message. This is particularly useful when you get an unexpected reaction from the person you are communicating with—a big clue that a misunderstanding is in the making. Suppose you enter a room where two of your friends are talking. They abruptly stop talking when they see you. One of them frowns and the other turns her back toward you. From these nonverbal cues, you think that you have interrupted a serious personal discussion about you and your friends are mad at you. Don't just turn around and leave assuming you are unwanted. Say, "I'm sorry, I didn't mean to interrupt. Should I leave"? Your perception may be confirmed if they ask you to come back later. On the other hand, they may have been arguing about something, and what you saw was directed at each other. They may in fact be very glad to see you so they have a reason to stop their argument or have you as a neutral party to help resolve their conflict.

What happens when you try to get confirmation and you get conflicting messages? In other words, the verbal message says one thing and the nonverbal cues imply something else? For example: You ask your significant other if she will help you study for your biology exam. She says, "Okay, I will." However the nonverbal cues (a big sigh accompanied by a look at the clock) leads you to believe she really doesn't want to help you. Try to confirm your interpretation by saying, "You said Okay, but it seems like you really don't want to right now." If she raises the volume of her voice, rolls her eyes and says, "I said (stressing with their voice the word said) I'd help!" you are faced with contradicting messages, one verbal and one nonverbal. Which do you believe? Most people would probably believe the nonverbal cue and decide to study alone. While you can't always confirm your perceptions before you act on them, trying to verify them when possible leads to more effective communication.

Conclusion

We must consider that there are many factors that constitute nonverbal communication. Nonverbal cues, such as use of space, clothing, and facial expressions, are not words, but they send a powerful message. How we interpret another person's nonverbal cues is important to mutual understanding. Why might he be using that tone with you? Is the tone really directed at you, or is he having a bad day? Are you being influenced by a person's clothes or hair? Has the person moved too close to you and are you uncomfortable? Have you ever sat across from someone whose posture is stiff? What does that mean? Answering any and all of these questions can help you become aware of nonverbal cues so you can interpret them more precisely. We must strive to understand nonverbal communication so that our communication can be more clear and effective.

We also must have an awareness of the nonverbal cues that we use. We must treat each communication experience as unique and be aware of the power of our nonverbal communication. To be understood and to communicate more effectively, we must skillfully use and interpret nonverbal communication. This is another key to survival.

DISCUSSION QUESTIONS

1. Since nonverbal communication is ambiguous, how can you verify your interpretations of someone else's message? Use a personal example.

2. Describe a situation you have experienced where the real meaning of a message was conveyed with nonverbal communication rather than with the words that were used.

3. Describe a situation that you were in where nonverbal communication contradicted the verbal communication. Which did you believe? Why?

4. What is meant by "You cannot NOT communicate"?

5. Since many nonverbal cues are culturally based, what problems could arise if you travel or interact with people raised in a culture different from yours?

6. Describe a situation where a first impression you had turned out to be incorrect or caused a misunderstanding. Has anyone's first impression of you caused a misunderstanding? If so, explain the circumstances.

KEY TERMS

affect display
artifacts
emblems
illustrators
intimate space
nonverbal cues

paralanguage
personal space
proxemics
public space
social space
territoriality

chapter four

Listening

Huh? Were you talking to me?

CHAPTER HIGHLIGHTS

- Hearing is not listening.

- Listening occurs in a sequential process.

- This process involves five stages: hearing, attending, evaluating, retaining, and responding.

- Nonlistening can be troublesome and costly.

- There are many reasons why we don't listen.

- These reasons can contribute to repetitive behaviors or habits.

- Effective listening reduces poor habits and has many benefits.

- We can become an effective listener by learning to develop our listening skills.

- There are three listening styles we can learn.

- Using these styles correctly can help us to become better listeners.

Jason still could not believe that Susan had not come to the train station. He tried to remember all the details of their phone conversation earlier that day. He had phoned and told Susan to meet him at the station at five. He had also stressed that she should not be late. She had sounded annoyed. Her tone was abrupt and she had talked very quickly. Maybe she hadn't heard him say the time. Maybe she wasn't listening. Sometimes Susan would tune him out completely when a client or someone else was in the room. Maybe that had happened this time. Jason was frustrated and depressed. The train sped on with Jason moping unhappily in his seat.

Susan wasn't very happy. She was thinking about her phone conversation with Jason. He had called at a very busy time. She knew she had sounded sharp with him. Sometimes when he called and she was busy, she had to ask him to repeat information because a client or coworker was also talking to her in the background. If there were too many things happening, Susan's brain would just shut down. Sometimes Jason would get annoyed and say things like "Did you hear me? You never listen to me!" "Aren't you paying any attention to what I am saying?" "I know you heard me! Answer me!" Jason was going to think she had tuned him out and wasn't paying attention again. No wonder he didn't wait for her, she thought. What should she do now? She would wait awhile and try to call his cell phone and apologize. Susan was miserable. What a day!

What Is Listening?

Does any of this sound familiar? Chances are it does. Listening to others is an important element in our lives. That is why we have two ears and only one mouth! It is also one of the communication skills we take for granted. We tend to assume that if we hear something we have listened. Nothing could be further from the truth. Understanding the difference between hearing and listening is a good way to begin our study of this very important skill.

As defined in chapter 1, *hearing* is the physical process of receiving messages. Hearing occurs when sound waves strike the eardrum. This causes a signal to be sent through the nervous system to the brain. The brain registers this signal as sound. However, this process does not insure that the sound has been listened to. *Listening* is the psychological process of trying to understand the message you have just heard. Listening involves a conscious effort to pay attention so that you can understand what is being said. Obviously you cannot listen to something you haven't heard, but you hear many things and don't listen. Listening is an important process in communication.

The Listening Process

As we have learned, hearing is not listening. In fact, hearing is actually only the first step of the listening process. Listening actually occurs in five stages, the other four being attending, evaluating, retaining, and responding. As we complete a stage, we advance onward in the process to the next stage, and so on.

All five stages must occur sequentially before we can say that listening has occurred. The process can break down during any stage, and we often complete only stage one, hearing, before immediately responding. We hear something and nod (respond) because we know from the signal received in our brain that sound has occurred. We do not wish to look like we weren't paying attention, so we provide feedback with a shake of our head. Unfortunately, the sender of the message assumes that we listened to him and moves on to his next point. We are left with a misunderstanding or, worse, nothing, because we did not listen properly. Let's examine what happens at each of the five stages in the listening process. This will help us when we begin our discussion on how to become a better listener.

- **Stage One: Hearing.** Hearing is the physical process of receiving sound. This special sense allows us to receive noises and tones as stimuli. We know that this is the stage in which sound waves received from our external atmosphere are sent to the brain: Sound is experienced when energy is transmitted through the air. This transmission serves as a stimulus to the ears. When we experience this process, hearing occurs. The brain receives the sound and begins to process the stimuli. Unless you have a physical hearing defect, all of us hear when this process occurs. Whether or not we listen depends on getting to the next stage in the process, attending.

- *Stage Two: Attending.* Once the brain has processed the sound stimuli and emitted the signal that hearing has occurred, we must choose to pay attention to the sound waves that have been received. The listening process now reverts to a psychological process, and we make a conscious effort to pay attention to the speaker's voice. Once our attention is focused on the speaker, we must try to learn what the speaker means.

- *Stage Three: Evaluating.* Once we have made the conscious effort to pay attention to the sound received, we must attempt to understand or evaluate the message. When we evaluate a message we attempt to determine how important the information is or how it affects us. Often we compare new information to our prior experiences, or we evaluate the risk associated with accepting or denying the information. We often make a judgment about the information or the speaker based on these evaluations. Once this stage is completed, we need to remember our evaluation of the message. This leads us to stage four of the listening process.

- *Stage Four: Retaining.* Although this stage is wholly dependent on our ability to decipher meaning from the message and our evaluation of it, we will attempt to retain all or bits and pieces of the message. This retention process prepares our brain to recall this information rapidly over the short period of time we require to respond to a message. The power of the memory process is delicate. Some people have very reliable short-term memories. Other people have difficulty retaining information for even a very short period. This depends on the situation at hand and the type and amount of information being stored. The time in which past events are stored, no matter how short, must occur before the memory can be turned into a response. Remember our discussion of the model in chapter 1. Thoughts must be turned into images to create a message. These thoughts come from memory. Memory is dependent on the evaluation of information that occurs at stage three. If you have problems remembering things, don't be quick to assume it's because you have a poor memory. It is more likely because you don't listen! This process is definitely sequential, with one stage being totally and completely dependent on the stage that occurs previously. Once stage four has been completed, we can move to the fifth and final stage of the listening process, responding.

• *Stage Five: Responding.* In this final stage, we must provide a response to the sender of the message we have heard, paid attention to, evaluated, and remembered. This is the stage where we provide an answer or action that serves as a reply. We know this process is also called feedback from our discussion in chapter 1. Once we have completed this stage, listening has actually occurred.

Listening has not occurred if any of the stages are incomplete or missing; all five stages are required. Obviously, there are many things that can get in the way of our ability to listen to messages from others. The reasons why we don't listen can cause poor listening habits to develop over time. We will discuss the reasons we don't listen and the habits that can develop from these situations later. Let's first discuss why ineffective listening can be troublesome and ultimately costly.

Nonlistening Can Be Troublesome and Costly

Studies have shown that the average person spends approximately half of his or her communication time in situations that require listening. Therefore, listening is an important part of the interpersonal communication process. It can help us to create effective communication situations, strengthen our relationships, and make us more successful. Nonlistening can be troublesome. It results in ineffective communication, can be damaging to relationships, and can affect our ability to successfully complete other tasks.

One consequence of poor listening is that it will decrease the amount of information we process. Put very simply, this means that if you don't understand or remember because you didn't listen, then you can't learn new information. Poor listeners are less intelligent than good listeners because they have eliminated the sources from which they could learn.

Another problem that results from ineffective listening is misunderstandings. When we don't listen, we don't have a full understanding of what was said. Therefore, we may receive a very different message from the one that was intended. For example, you might have to fill out a form twice because you failed to listen when you were told to print, and used cursive instead. Nonlistening accounts for patients taking the wrong dose of medicine, students completing the wrong assignment, children missing curfews, and a traveler turning in the wrong direction. Nonlistening results in misunderstandings, which range from being mildly annoying to being deadly.

A third effect of nonlistening is an abundance of missed opportunities. When we fail to listen, we run the risk of losing out on an opportunity to go somewhere or to be involved in something. These opportunities may be small, such as missing out on a ball game or a party. They may be major, such as missing a job interview that can lead to financial gain or an opportunity for personal gain. Furthermore, when we fail to listen to others we often miss the chance to create or strengthen a relationship. Nonlistening is costly.

The cost of ineffective listening can be measured economically. It may be simple, such as a ruined dinner because you did not listen to instructions. A ruined dinner results in a trip to get fast food, costing time and money. How about booking airline tickets for the wrong day because you did not listen to your spouse say he could not travel on Friday? This nonlistening error is a lot more costly than a fast-food meal. Studies have concluded that simple listening mistakes in the workforce can cause billions of dollars in lost revenue by the time the mistake is found and corrected. Meetings have to be rescheduled, production lines may shut down, or products recalled, all of which uses time, and time is money. Nonlistening can cost big bucks!

Perhaps one of the most detrimental effects of poor listening is conflict. Problems between people often can be traced back to the failure to listen. These are the times we fail to get the whole message or assume we know what is being said and tune out. Arguments that develop can harm relationships.

As we can see, there are complications that can occur when we don't listen. All of them adversely affect communication, and some are very risky. Nonlistening can waste time, and incurs costs—both emotional and financial. Luckily, the reverse is also true. As listening behaviors improve, communication improves. About the only real risk of listening is that you may become aware of something you would rather not know, but knowledge of an event or emotion isn't detrimental. Most of the time knowing something and understanding what is happening is better than being unaware. We can deal with what we know much better than dealing with the fear and anxiety of the unknown.

You are now aware of the fact that there are many problems that can occur when you don't listen. In addition, nonlistening over time can cause poor habits to result. Understanding why we don't listen can help us break our poor listening habits.

Why We Don't Listen

If listening is so beneficial and virtually risk-free, then why do so few of us do it effectively? There are several answers to this question. We will examine reasons why we don't listen and the poor listening behaviors or habits that can develop. **Habits**, by definition, are behavior patterns that are acquired by frequent repetition. Most habits become so ingrained that

Activity for Further Understanding

Gossip

The purpose of this activity is to illustrate that most of us "hear" but do not listen. Your instructor will take a student out of the classroom and tell him or her a short story. The student will then repeat the message to the next person who comes out. The first student will then return to the class, sending another person out to hear the message. This process will continue until everyone has had a chance to hear and repeat the message. The last person to hear the message will write the message on the board. The instructor should write the original message below this message. Discuss the difference in the final message received and the original message sent. What happened and why? Did any distractions get in the way? Did they result in any poor listening habits occurring and interfering with the message?

The Rules

1. Repeat the message exactly as you received it.
2. Repeat the message once and only once when you are the sender.
3. Do not write down the message you received before sending it on to the next person.

Listening is a skill, and just like any other skill, it can be learned. You can listen if you can hear, but that doesn't mean it is easy to listen. To become a more effective listener we must become aware of when we aren't listening. Discovering why we aren't listening can help us to better understand what behaviors need to be improved. With dedication, awareness, and some useful practical steps you can reap the benefits of becoming a more effective listener.

we simply do them without thinking about them. You get up in the morning, stumble into the bathroom, and start brushing your teeth. Mary gets up every morning and has the "habit" of drinking a diet cola instead of coffee. Why? Repetitive behavior done over and over again is the factor causing the act to become a habit. The same is true about how and when you listen or choose not to listen.

The reasons that lead to nonlistening have quite simply caused us to develop the repetitive pattern of poor listening behaviors, therefore becoming habits for most of us. They are so ingrained that we aren't even aware of the fact that we are not listening to those around us. Habits are difficult to change because of the very fact that we behave unconsciously. We are on autopilot, and our mind is contemplating something different from what we are doing. Have you ever been driving and suddenly realized you're at your destination but don't remember passing any of the familiar landmarks? Why? You were on autopilot. Becoming a more effective listener will require you to be aware of the times you become distracted. You'll need to turn the "autopilot" off. You will have to attempt to become aware of your nonlistening episodes and understand what causes them so that poor habits are not formed.

We Like to Talk

Although most of us intellectually know that interpersonal communication requires speakers and listeners, most of us concentrate on talking. Our desire to speak and press our own opinions becomes a distraction to the listening process. While someone else is talking, we find our thoughts drifting to what we want to say. Consequently, we quit listening or fail to listen at all. This love of expressing our own ideas and hearing our own voice can be traced to the fact that in society talking seems to be emphasized more than listening. This can lead to the poor habit of **stage hogging**, or interrupting another speaker so you can express your own views or opinions. Think about it. From the time we are born we are encouraged to talk. "Say dada, say mama." Our parents wonder what our first words will be. "Aly said bye-bye today, what a good girl! Mommy and Daddy are so proud of her!" Not until much later, if ever, do we consider whether the child is listening. At parties, the person talking and joking is perceived to be the life of the party, while the person sitting and listening is labeled a wallflower, or worse, a bore. Observe the political process in our country. Who gets elected to office? Is it the person who is great at giving speeches, or the person who simply listens and says very little? Obviously, it is the speaker who is happy on election night. Because speaking has been overly emphasized in our society, we have grown up with the impression that speaking is better than listening. This has caused many of us to believe that interjecting our viewpoint in a conversation is necessary. This is how the poor habit of stage hogging originates. Stage hoggers give you the impression that what they have to say is far more important than what you have to say. If someone is constantly interrupting others she cannot be listening.

We Allow Assumptions and Biases to Intrude

Another barrier to listening occurs because of our personal environments. Recall that personal environment consists of all the experiences we have had from the day we were born. These experiences are stored in our brain and shape our personalities and behaviors. We bring our environment with us to any communication interaction; it is a part of us, because it is us! Unfortunately, not all of the events we have experienced in our lives have been positive. We have experiences that we would rather not repeat, and some have been so negative that they have caused us to form undesirable impressions about events, people, or situations. These impressions become assumptions or biases.

Assumptions are ideas that we accept as true without needing any proof. **Biases** are our inclination to be in favor of or against something based on our unsupported assumptions. Assumptions and biases are two of the reasons why we don't listen. They are the most detrimental of all the barriers to listening, and they can lead to **prejudice**, that is, an irrational attitude of hostility directed at an individual or group. When we are prejudicial, we tend not to listen to any information that may contradict our beliefs. Assumptions and biases also cause us to develop the poor habit of **assimilation.** When we assimilate, we compare new information with prior information already stored in our heads. If the new information does not match with prior information already stored, we reject it and stop listening to any further information. This causes us to tune out when we hear messages that we do not agree with, or that don't fit what we already believe or assume to be true. Picture yourself in the following situations and examine the probable outcomes.

> Your girlfriend is telling you about her problem with her boss. Since you have heard her discuss this topic almost every day for a week, you *assume* you don't need to listen and tune out. Instead, she has told you that she was fired today; you weren't listening. What happens next?

> You are sitting in your Algebra class and, as usual, you are totally lost. You cease to listen to the lecture because you *assume* it is too difficult for you to understand anyway. Math has never been your thing and you know you will fail. However, this time, the instructor was announcing extra credit and tutoring available to students experiencing problems. You tuned out because you assumed you knew what he was going to say. What have you missed?

> Finally, there is a discussion on TV between two senators who have opposite views on gun control. You are against laws governing the purchase and use of guns. The senator who favors gun-control legislation is speaking. Because of your *bias*, you may not even listen to the speaker. If you choose to listen, you might assimilate what the senator says and decide to reject the information because it does not fit with your views, or you might believe the speaker has said something she didn't, or you might add messages that weren't really included. You tune out; you don't listen. Your assumptions and biases will continue to give you an excuse not to listen. Have you missed an opportunity?

None of what has been said is intended to imply that assumptions and biases are necessarily wrong. Everyone forms them, and they are desirable at times. The point is, when they cause us to assimilate and interfere with our listening, we could miss out on useful information. These habits can negatively affect the entire communication process.

Tracey's uncle had a sign on his desk that looked like this, ASS/U/ME. When asked what this meant he would reply, "Every time you assume you make an ass out of you and me." It has always been a rather graphic reminder to her to listen first and apply assumptions later, if at all.

We Are Distracted by "Noise"

Another reason we don't listen was also introduced in chapter 1. We do not listen because we are easily distracted. We called these distractions noise; it occurs externally and internally and interferes with listening. External noise includes those distractions like the TV, loud machinery, children crying, or even an uncomfortable chair. Noises that occur externally to the body make it difficult to pay attention. They can even make it difficult to hear. Take the phone off the hook, turn off the CD player, or tell the kids to play outside. In other words, get rid of distractions that you can control in your immediate external environment and focus on listening instead.

Internal noise is that which occurs inside our bodies, such as talking to ourself in our head, our stomach growling because we are hungry, or being overly tired. A student provided an example of internal noise that may be quite familiar to most of us. She usually gets home from classes at about 2:30 in the afternoon, and her 10-year-old son arrives at 3:00. As he is telling her about his day's activities and plans, the dog barks, her stomach growls because she's hungry, and she is tired from a full day at school. She's bombarded by noise. She tries to listen, but the barking dog causes her to think about letting him out, her growling stomach causes her to want to fix supper, and her tired body causes her to want a nap. She wants to listen, and even tries to listen, but these noises or distractions prevent her from doing so. She only listens to part of what her son is saying and tunes the rest out. Noise has caused her to develop the poor habit of selective listening.

Selective listening occurs when we choose, or select, those parts of a message that we want to listen to. We then tune everything else out. We are so busy in any given day that most of us display this poor habit on a regular basis. Unfortunately, when we hear only part of a message, we do not get a clear understanding of what is being communicated, and this can have disastrous results. In the case of our student, her son was so used to his mom tuning him out that he began to come home from school, say hi, and then close himself in his room to play video games. For a while he didn't bother to speak to her at all!

Another interruption that can occur during the listening process is a form of internal noise called **preoccupation**. Preoccupation is the noise caused by your own internal thoughts, your intrapersonal communication. Daydreaming about the weekend and thinking about your chemistry test during your English class are examples of preoccupation. When we are preoccupied with our own thoughts, we find it difficult to listen to others.

We Get Too Much Information

We are often so overwhelmed with thoughts that our brains just shut down. This can lead to the poor listening habit of **message overload**. A good way to understand this concept is to think of your electrical appliances. If you had your computer, television, stereo, toaster, and coffee maker all plugged into the same outlet, you would probably blow a fuse. In most homes you would not be able to use any of these appliances until you located the fuse box and fixed the blown circuit. You then would have to relocate your electrical items so they did not plug into the same outlet. This would require a definite conscious action to start things rolling again. The same is true of message overload if it occurs during the listening process. If you are overwhelmed with thoughts and your brain "blows" a fuse, shutting down, it takes a conscious effort to start the listening process back up. If we allow information overload to become a habit, it may consistently distract us from tuning in to important messages. Information swirling around in your head can always be put aside and returned to later, but chances are the person speaking will not be repeating his message again. In theory, correcting this problem is fairly simple, just flip the switch, but in reality it isn't always that easy to focus. Obviously the point is to concentrate on the message being sent and postpone thinking about what is on your mind until later when it can be retrieved. Nothing is lost and you have gained new information from focusing on the message.

We Think Faster than We Speak

The rate at which we speak and think is another culprit that distracts us from listening. People are capable of understanding speech at a rate four to five times faster than the average person actually speaks. This discrepancy in our **speaking/thinking rate** means our brains get bored. The boredom causes our brains to go on vacation if someone is speaking too slowly. We have a tendency to use this spare time to let our minds wander and become preoccupied with our own thoughts, thus we fail to pay attention to the speaker. Our brains tune in and out, catching only bits and pieces of what the speaker is saying. We don't get the full picture or context of the message. We don't complete all five steps in the listening process. This leads to the poor listening habit of **filling in the gaps**. When we haven't listened because our minds drifted due to boredom, we don't get all of the facts. When we attempt to respond to the speaker, we don't know enough information. We must make up information to fill in the gaps to account for the details we have missed. However, this often causes misunderstandings because our response is based on false data that we have made up or imagined. When this becomes a habit, it can cause ongoing communication problems.

If you recognize these behaviors (and we believe you will), then you will have taken the first step toward improving your listening skills. Being aware of our actual behavior is an important step to understanding why we do what we do. Having a clear understanding of the reasons you fail to listen, and the poor habits that can result, will allow you to improve your listening skills.

The Benefits of Learning to Listen

Learning to listen is a skill. We don't listen because *we aren't trained to listen.* Did you ever take a class devoted to teaching you how to listen effectively? Did your parents ever sit you down and say, "Okay, this is what you do to listen"? Probably not, even though there are the infrequent lessons on listening taught to music majors, or active listening taught to nursing or psychology majors. Yet, even these courses don't actually teach students listening skills. Most of us assume that if we can hear we listen. We've got two ears and have been listening for years; we don't have to study it, right? Wrong! We have learned that hearing is not listening. Many things distract us. We believe we are listening because we "hear" sound. Most of us think we are relatively skilled listeners for this reason. The fact is that while everyone engages in listening, few do it well. Studies have shown that when people are asked to rate how well they listen on a scale of one (low) to ten (high) the average person will rate herself a seven on that scale. When these same people are actually tested, and unaware their listening is being evaluated, the average score is a three. The number of participants scoring five or above is so small that these individuals are considered to be exceptional listeners! In fact, many studies confirm that we only listen to about half of what we hear in any given day!

The previous exercise helps you identify the people, situations, and topics that trigger your ineffective listening. Chances are these behaviors have led to the development of poor listening habits. It may be difficult at first to catch yourself not listening, but if you are determined to improve your communication with others, you can do it. You *can* become an effective listener. Effective listening has many benefits.

Studies show that students who listen, effectively, improve their grades. The added benefit of earning better grades in school will also increase your job opportunities and future success. One reward for listening is success at work and school. Numerous surveys of employers and managers have overwhelmingly rated listening as the number one communication skill necessary for job success. Improving your listening skills can increase your chance for employment, improve your job skills, lead to promotions, and add to your economic security.

Another benefit of listening is improved interpersonal relationships. Just as poor listening skills lead to problems between people, good listen-

Activity for Further Understanding

Nonlistening Journal

This activity will help you recognize when you aren't listening. Once your poor behaviors are identified, you can begin to make any necessary changes.

1. For several days keep track of your nonlistening behaviors. There will be several times each day that you fail to listen to what is said. Collect ten examples of these situations.

2. For each of your nonlistening situations, do the following:

   a. Describe the situation by stating who was speaking and what you remember about the message sent.

   b. Explain what distraction occurred and what you did instead of listening. Label the distraction appropriately; noise, preoccupation, bias.

   c. State the poor habit that occurred because you didn't listen: selective listening, etc.

3. After completing step two, review and summarize what you have learned about your own ineffective listening behavior. Are there any patterns to your nonlistening? Are there particular topics or people that tend to distract you? What is the general outcome when you fail to really listen? What poor habit, if any, is primary for you?

ing skills help to improve relationships. You need no surveys or studies to prove this point. All you have to do is think about the last time someone really listened to you. He didn't interrupt you with his own opinions; his comments showed he understood what you said. He may not necessarily have agreed with you, but he listened and it felt good. One of the biggest problems in relationships is that we think others aren't listening to us. This hurts our feelings and often generates a breakdown in the relationship. Need a boost to a relationship? Try listening more and talking less. The better we become at listening, the less likely we are to miss information that will keep us from making mistakes in our relationships.

The effects of good listening are infinite. The risks involved in becoming a more effective listener are almost nonexistent. Improving your listening skills can only result in positive consequences. Let's discuss some ways that you can become a better listener.

Becoming a Better Listener

Learning different styles of listening can help you become a better listener. These listening styles can be very effective in communication. In some circumstances you may wish to use one specific listening style, while in others you may find it more effective to use a combination of the different styles to help you understand the message you hear. The three listening styles are: **deliberate listening**, **empathic listening**, and **participatory listening**. The following discussion will help explain the process of each style and give you an idea of how they are most effectively used and why they can improve your listening skills.

- *Deliberate Listening.* The act of listening for a specific purpose, deliberate listening requires the process of slow and careful thought, weighing facts and arguments. The purpose of this type of listening is to extract important information from a message. Deliberate listening is used most effectively in situations where the data we are receiving has a specific purpose or use. In other words, the speaker is attempting to convey information in a clear and straightforward manner. When your boss is telling you what you need to do for the day, your teacher is reviewing information that will be on an exam, or your mom is giving you a grocery list, deliberate listening is effective. A deliberate listener must not become a selective listener, listening only for what he thinks is important or interesting, because this would interfere with the outcome or goal of the message. For this reason, deliberate listening is most effective when used in situations that are not emotionally charged and when the message is fairly factual. Deliberate listening is primarily a method for obtaining information that is sent verbally without much emotion attached.

- *Empathic Listening.* The process of understanding not only the words that are said, but also *how* the words are said, is the idea behind empathic listening. Empathic listening requires us to see the meaning behind the words. Most people only focus on the actual words of a message. But as we have learned in the chapter on nonverbal communication, how we say what we say can also send a very powerful message. Empathic listening requires the listener to "listen" to both the verbal and nonverbal elements of the message in order to analyze the emotion behind the message. Empathic listening is needed in situations where the emotional content of the message is just as important as the words being said in order to understand what the speaker is really conveying. When your child is crying over something you think is no big deal, when your mom is angry because you forgot to take out the trash, or when your best friend complains that you don't have time for her anymore, empathic listening is appropriate. Indeed, in situations that are emotionally charged for the speaker, it is not only effective to use this style, it is almost necessary in order to understand what is really being communicated.

Empathic listeners try to put themselves in the other person's shoes. They attempt to put themselves in the speaker's place to get a better idea of what a person is saying and feeling. Empathy doesn't require you to agree with what is being said, it only requires you to acknowledge another person's perspective. When you listen empathetically, you focus on the speaker and temporarily set aside your own viewpoint. When you have fully understood the message, and the other person agrees that you understand what was meant, you can look at the whole picture. The Cherokee saying, "Don't judge a man until you have walked a mile in his moccasins," is the idea behind empathic listening. It is an effective communication tool.

- *Participatory Listening.* This listening technique requires that the listener participate with the speaker when she sends a message by repeating what she has communicated. This method of repeating back is called **paraphrasing** and is used to help verify understanding. Paraphrasing is repeating, in your own words, what you believe the speaker has said. This in turn gives the speaker an opportunity to verify or correct your perception. Participatory listening can be used in many different listening situations. An excellent time to use this type of listening is in a classroom. We know that we would like our students to use this method more often! You can paraphrase what you understand your instructor to have said. For example, say, "You are now saying there are four types of models. I only remember three." If you are confused, this method gives the instructor a much better idea of how to help than a muttered, "I don't get it." Participatory listening is also effective when you are being given instructions, when you are trying to achieve a solution to a problem, or when you are trying to understand why someone is treating you a certain way. When you paraphrase, be careful not to "parrot" the speaker's words back to her word for word. Put the ideas, as you understand them, into your own words and then ask the speaker if both of you share the same meaning.

  Participatory listening is also used effectively to help others problem-solve. It can help the speaker examine the problem more objectively. When your son is concerned about his batting average and wants to talk, when your spouse says she has a problem at work, or when your best friend wants to talk to you about his problem with his girlfriend, participatory listening and paraphrasing are very effective. Having the opportunity to listen to you paraphrase their circumstances allows the other person to step away from the problem and also shows that you are really listening, making the person feel supported.

These three listening styles are not always easy to use, and they are certainly not automatic for many of us. However, when used correctly, and in the proper situations, they become easier.

Conclusion

We live in a world where we communicate during a large percentage of our day. We do so by both speaking and listening. Remember not to assume that if we hear, we have listened. Listening involves much more than simply hearing what is said. In fact, hearing is only the first step of the listening process. This process can be interrupted in many ways. Listening, as with all communication skills, needs to be monitored. This will insure that we avoid developing poor listening habits. If poor habits do or have developed, we will need to pay even closer attention in order to change our behavior. Breaking old habits may not be easy, but the payoff is great. Our listening style should be adjusted to the situation at hand. Learning to be a more effective listener is key to our survival.

DISCUSSION QUESTIONS

1. Explain the difference between hearing and listening.
2. Discuss the concept of noise and how it affects the listening process.
3. What do you believe are the two reasons you fail to listen most often? What poor habits have you developed due to these behaviors?
4. Why would participatory listening help you explain your understanding of a message?
5. Is listening effectively more important than speaking effectively? Support your answer.

KEY TERMS

assimilation
assumptions
biases
deliberate listening
empathic listening
filling in the gaps
habits
message overload

paraphrasing
participatory listening
prejudice
preoccupation
selective listening
speaking/thinking rate
stage hogging

chapter five

Self-Concept and Self-Esteem

Me and My Shadow . . . My Shadow and Me

CHAPTER HIGHLIGHTS

- Self-concept can be defined as the beliefs a person holds to be true about him- or herself.
- Self-esteem is how the person feels about these beliefs.
- There are four primary factors that affect our self-concept and self-esteem: authority figures, social comparisons, gender expectations, and cultural influences.
- Authority figures are those people who we allow to have control over us.
- We decide who we are through social comparisons, or comparing ourselves to others.
- We are influenced by societal expectations of gender, how we should behave as men and women.
- Cultural influences are embedded in us throughout our lives, beginning at birth.
- The self is subjective, and resists change.
- Our self-concept significantly impacts our communication.
- You can make positive changes to your self-concept.
- A positive self-concept leads to higher self-esteem.

Susan wanted to call Jason, but her mother had always taught her that women were not supposed to call men. Her best friend Jane says that you should make the man call you. That way you know that he really loves you enough to want to talk to you. Susan was confused. She didn't care who called whom. She loved Jason and wanted to find out why he had not met her like he had said he would. She wanted to call him and find out why he had not been at The Station. Sometimes she wished she weren't so scared of things. She wished she weren't shy and awkward when she had to confront a problem. Once in awhile she wished she could change who she was.

Jason went from room to room in his apartment. The voice in his head kept telling him to call Susan. His friend Tom had told him that men never call women after a fight or problem because that is what women expected. Tom said it was better to wait and let the woman mull things over. That way she appreciated the call more. Tom was his best buddy, but as Jason thought about that, he realized he wanted Susan to be that person now. Why should he care what other people, even Tom, think of him anyway? He was a mature, responsible person who could make his own decisions, wasn't he? He was going to call Susan and get this mess straightened out right now.

What Are Self-Concept and Self-Esteem?

Who am I? I am a mother, sister, daughter, and aunt. I am a father, brother, son, and uncle. What am I? I have moods, feelings, talents, and beliefs. I am smart, funny, athletic, and tall. I am short, chubby, clumsy, and shy. Who am I?

Each of us has asked ourselves this question at some time or another. Sometimes the answer comes easily, and at other times we are unsure of the answer. Knowing who we are is an important factor in communication. We all have a personal environment that consists of all the experiences that we have had since the day we were born. We determine how we experience the world around us from these experiences (see chapter 1). This personal environment also shapes our beliefs, attitudes, and values; our abilities; and our personality traits. When we categorize, label, and evaluate these qualities, we form our self-concept and self-esteem.

Self-concept is what you believe to be true about yourself. This includes both internal and external elements such as mental, physical, and emotional states. It includes who you think you are and what purpose you have in this world—the roles that you have in life. Once you have determined what is true about you and identified your multiple roles, you likely attach an emotional response or value to those beliefs. These feelings we attach to the roles that we play is called our self-esteem.

Self-esteem quite simply is how you feel about who you are—how much you value yourself. For example, if you believe yourself to be a good student, then "student" is the role, a part of your self-concept; the label "good" is a term that describes how you feel about yourself as a student, or your opinion of yourself in that position. This feeling measures your sense of self-worth and is your self-esteem.

We have a feeling of value that we attach to each role we have in life: good student, clumsy dancer, poor speller. We also attach a value to how we feel about ourselves overall. Even though you may feel that you are a good student, a good parent, and a good friend, you could still have a low opinion of yourself in general. This would mean you have low self-esteem, or that you don't place a high value on your worth as an individual. Why is this so?

There are many factors that affect our self-concept and ultimately our self-esteem. In fact, both are formed by so many different influences at any given time that the development of our self is an ongoing process. Let's take a look at the primary factors that influence our self-concept and self-esteem.

How Is Our Self-Concept Formed?

Everyone's self-concept is formed by many factors. All people will be affected by the *same* factors, but no one will react in exactly the same way to any one factor. The primary factors that affect who we think we are and how we feel about ourselves are authority figures, social comparisons, gender expectations, and cultural influences. Let's examine each of these factors more closely.

Authority Figures

We may not want to believe that anyone has authority over us, and in fact no one can truly control us. However, there are people in our lives whom we allow to have significant influence and control. We might allow these people to make decisions for us or even allow them to tell us "who" we are. We give these people tremendous power and authority in our daily lives. These people are called **authority figures** and may include parents, significant others, bosses, teachers, or anyone else whom we allow to influence us in some way. Let's explore the two primary categories of authority figures: parents and significant others. Examining them will give us a better understanding of how they can significantly influence our self-concept.

Parents

For clarity, we will define **parents** as the person or persons who raised you from infancy. This may be two biological parents, but does not exclusively refer to birth parents. Our parents may be adoptive, a single parent, grandparents, aunts, uncles, or any number of other custodial guardians. Whomever we spent the majority of our time with during our early growth and development will be considered our parents for the purpose of discussing how they affect our self-concept. What do these people have to do with how we think about ourselves?

Simply stated, they influence us by everything they say and do. They become the mirror in which we see ourselves. Their opinions and actions become a **reflected appraisal** of how we see ourselves as well. When we are infants, our only method of communication is nonverbal. We use sounds because we don't know words. We cry because we are hungry, tired, or uncomfortable. How our parents react to these displays for attention, even at this early age, begins to tell us how others feel toward us. If our needs are met promptly and with affection, we will begin to form a positive self-concept. We believe we are important and valued. As we grow and begin to understand more of the world around us, we become even more aware of how our parents feel about us. If they treat us in a manner that implies they accept us and believe us to be good people, we will believe that about ourselves as well.

Remember that communication doesn't have to be verbal. In fact, actions truly do speak louder than words. For example, a student was asked to write a short paper about the effect his parents had on his self-concept. After class he came to the instructor and said, "I don't know what to write. My parents hardly ever talked to me." After an awkward moment of silence, he continued, "I guess that did tell me a lot, didn't it?" Communication doesn't have to be aimed directly at the child for it to affect his or her self-concept. For example, look at the scenario of a mom visiting her friend while three-year-old Marie plays on the floor.

> *Friend:* Marie plays so nicely and quietly. You must not have much
> of a problem with her.
>
> *Mom:* Yeah, well, she's my shy one. Her brothers are more outgo-
> ing, but at least she isn't much of a bother.

Marie has ears, and what her mother just said will affect how she perceives herself, particularly if it is repeated on a frequent basis. She will begin to believe she is shy, based on her mother's judgment of her. Her mother's opinion (appraisal) is projected (reflected) onto her, and she begins to accept it as the truth.

Our parents' influence doesn't stop when we turn 5, 18, or even 80. We are continually influenced by their opinions during our lifetime. Many people react to how their parents would have responded to their behavior even after their parents have died and are unable to communicate acceptance or rejection. We frequently remain tied to our parents' beliefs when we are mature adults. The degree of a parent's influence on self-concept will vary from person to person and may shift in importance throughout our lives, but their effect is apparent on all of us.

Significant Others

Significant others are a special category of people that may include extended family members, teachers, clergy, day-care providers, coworkers, and others. Usually these are people other than our parents whom we see on a regular basis and are involved in some way in our lives. These are people whose opinions are those we respect and from whom we want approval. If they give us their approval and confirm our feelings of self-worth, we will develop a more positive self-image. The opposite is true as well. Significant others can (and often do) influence us as much as (and sometimes more than) our parents.

The power we give to significant others changes as we age, as does the person who is our primary significant other. When we are young, our primary significant other may be a parent or a playmate. As we grow older and enter school, this person may be a teacher or a principal. As we age and form more intimate relationships, this person could be our fiancé or our spouse.

While significant others are people with whom we regularly interact, this interaction doesn't necessarily have to be face-to-face or even reciprocal. Significant others can be people with whom we chat online or exchange e-mail or can even be an actor on TV. In fact, the media greatly influence self-concept. A large percentage of our time is spent with the media. Studies show that children enter kindergarten with thousands of hours of video and television viewing experiences. Radio is a constant companion in most of our cars, and billboards flash by our windows. Every year the music industry takes in billions of dollars from the sale of CDs, and print media (on- and off-line) is available everywhere. We spend so much of our time with all types of media that the media become a significant other, impacting a large portion of our daily lives. For example, we determine whether we are wearing stylish clothing or whether we are driving the right automobile based on messages we receive from the media.

Social Comparisons

We see ourselves through the people we become involved with and through broader society as well. How we fit into society and how we perceive our relationship to it affects our self-concept. While the effect general society has on you may not be as significant as the effect your parents may have had, it does exist. As you examine who you perceive yourself to be and how you feel about yourself, consider how you compare yourself to others—how you make **social comparisons**.

Peers

A **peer** is someone who is very similar to us. Usually, our peers are approximately our age and are of the same economic and social status. Peers can also include our colleagues, those people who are involved in the same profession or share the same interests even if demographic characteristics are not the same. For example, all your classmates are your peers to a certain extent. They may be of various ages and from different backgrounds, but your shared experience in communication class makes them your peers.

Suppose Noah is taking piano lessons while the rest of the neighborhood children are playing softball. When he is asked to play ball, he replies that he has to practice the piano and can't join in the game. The reactions of his peers will affect how he perceives himself. If they indicate to Noah that they understand practicing the piano is of value, he will be more likely to view himself positively. If they respond by teasing him, indicating their disdain for playing the piano, he will likely view himself negatively.

As we age, many of our peers become a reference or comparison group by which we gauge how well we think we are doing in society. These peers become known as our **referent group**, and they exert tremendous pressure for us to excel. They are responsible for what most people experience as adult "peer" pressure. Traditionally, peer influence (usually referred to as "peer pressure") has been associated with teenagers. Although it is certainly true that during the ages of 12–19 we seem to be preoccupied with how our friends accept or view something, peer pressure continues throughout our lives.

Let's say you have a perfectly respectable car. It runs well and looks fairly good, but is 10 years old. Suddenly, your neighbors and friends all seem to have new cars. If you compare your car to theirs, it is probably safe to assume that you may feel your car is not acceptable. This affects your self-concept. You might feel you need a new car to be viewed as successful and accepted by your neighbors. Everyone is not equally affected by peer pressure and a desire to look good in the eyes of their peers. However, to one extent or another, most people compare themselves with people whom they believe are similar to themselves.

Groups

Another significant factor that plays a role in how we view ourselves is group membership. We live in a society that is filled with people who share similar activities or interests. People who join together due to these similar interests or activities form a **group**. Stop for a moment and think about all of the groups you belong to. Your list may include a baseball team, church choir, student council, PTA, archery club, bowling team, or Rotary club. When we become a member of a group, we are expected to conform to the rules and norms of that group. We are often ranked and judged according to how well we function as a member within these same groups. For example, if you bowl regularly, maintaining a high average would be important to you. A perfect score in bowling is 300, or 12 consecutive strikes in one game. If you do not bowl that well, and most people don't, then you are assigned a handicap based on the average score that you have received for all of the games you have bowled. This number is used in a ranking system to compare you to other bowlers. We are "compared" to others in similar ways anytime we become a member of some group. As a student you have a G.P.A., or grade point average. This number compares you to other students at the university that you attend and ranks how well you perform as a student. If you are president of the Rotary club, you "outrank" other officers such as the treasurer or secretary. Our society is loaded with groups. How you function within these groups affects your self-concept. Group social roles have a significant impact on who you think you are and how you feel about yourself.

Gender Expectations

In addition to comparisons imposed by society, we are also influenced by societal expectations of how we should behave as men and women. We will devote an entire chapter (7) to this later, for now it is important to understand that our self-concept is affected by how well we function as a man or woman in society. For example, we are conditioned into male and female roles from birth: boys roll in the dirt, play with bugs, ride bikes, and wrestle; girls play house, feed baby dolls, dress up, and fix hair. Boys are conditioned to be tough; think of the nursery rhyme that says boys are made of snips and snails, and puppy dog tails. Girls are similarly conditioned to be soft; sugar and spice, and everything nice, that's what girls are made of. In fact, take a look at advertising today. The media promote these gender-specific images regularly, and since boys and girls are exposed to television and other media at such an early age, they are influenced by media messages as well. What happens when we don't fit the role imposed by these societal expectations? If a little girl wants to play in the dirt, she is told her behavior is not lady-like, and she is often punished and directed into some other activity. The same is true of a small boy who wishes to feed the "baby." He may be told that this is "sissy" behavior and then given a truck to play with. These societal messages have a tremendous impact on how we view ourselves as normal functioning men and women. If a woman does not want to nurture, and a man does, they are rejecting the societal norm for their gender. How we accept and fit within societal norms with regard to gender affects our self-concept.

Cultural Influences

We are significantly influenced throughout our lives by our external surroundings and our home environment. How we are raised and how we grow up has an impact on who we think we are. Our culture, which includes values and beliefs, molds our thinking and behavior and influences how well we function in society. This in turn will have an impact on our self-concept and self-esteem. If you grew up in the south, your values and lifestyle are likely different from someone who grew up in the north. If you grew up on a farm, your culture is different from someone raised in the city. Growing up in the United States (as opposed to an Eastern country) molds us to behave in certain ways that are acceptable and expected in Western cultures. For example, the United States is an individualistic society. In other countries, such as Japan, cultural influences have produced a collectivist society. These types of orientations influence our self-concept.

In an individualistic society, importance is placed on being independent—self-sufficient. We put emphasis on the self as a single entity. While group membership may be used to judge an individual's prestige, it is the *person* who is being praised or put down and typically not the group. In such a society, being self-sufficient—able to think and act based upon personal decisions—is valued. These types of evaluations are the type of social comparisons that affect our self-concept and self-esteem. They are vastly different than the expectations given to people in a collectivist society.

Collectivist societies link an individual's identity with his family and with the group he belongs to. It is the "we" rather than the "I" that is emphasized. You are expected to take care of "we" before "I." Rewards and punishments are shared equally among group members. The collectivist societies value age, tradition, and hierarchy. You are expected to conform to the rules of order within your group and are expected to perform your role in the group based on the status that same group affords you. Your actions reflect the entire group. Furthermore, you as a group member represent the entire group to people who are not in the group. For example, if you are caught cheating you bring shame to your entire family, not just yourself.

Although as a whole we are an individualistic society in the United States, there are those subgroups or families that function with the mentality of collectivist groups. The expectations and cultural influences of these families will have an impact on the self-concept of their individual family members.

Now that you are familiar with the different factors that influence self-concept, it is time to look specifically at your own beliefs. Through an examination of your personal beliefs, and their origin, you can begin to more fully understand yourself and ultimately improve your communication.

While it is important to realize factors that have had an effect on forming your self-concept, it is more important to realize that it is *your* self-concept. You and you alone are responsible for what you believe about yourself. Others can contribute their opinions about you and your behav-

 Activity for Further Understanding

Self-Beliefs

This activity will enable you to take a closer look at your "self." It will help you clarify how you perceive yourself and where this perception might have originated.

1. Write a description of how you perceive yourself in each of the following categories:

   a. physical characteristics (do you see yourself as short, thin, blonde, muscular?)

   b. relationships (what relationships are you the most involved in: spouse, children, sibling, friend?)

   c. social skills (are you outgoing, withdrawn, talkative?)

   d. talents (what are you good at or what would you like to be good at: music, mechanics, swimming, speaking?)

   e. strongly-held beliefs (are you pro-life, Christian, a political activist?)

   f. intellectual ability (are you good at math, science, spelling, Spanish?)

2. After writing these descriptions, take a look at what you wrote. Are these statements really true? Where did they come from (reflected appraisals or social comparisons)? Are any of them old? Write a summary of what you've learned.

3. As an addition to this activity, have someone else you know answer these same questions about you and then compare his/her answers with yours.

iors, and they can even influence your attitude about yourself. However, it is your perception of yourself that forms your self-concept. No matter how often people tell you what they think your capabilities are, it doesn't become part of your self-concept until you believe it. Blaming parents or society for how you feel or what you are is denying your responsibility to yourself. If there is something about yourself that you do not like, blaming someone else will not change it. Only you can make a better you. Your self-concept—who you think you are, and your self-esteem—how you feel about yourself, are the products of your own mind. Other factors can be influential, but it is you and you alone who decides what you will make part of you.

Characteristics of the Self

Being aware of our self-concept and our self-esteem is the first step in achieving more effective communication. However, our self-concept and self-esteem are not static. Depending on the moment or particular context, one day we may feel very positive about ourselves and our lives; the next day, we may be less confident. It is important that we frequently review our positive and negative self-perceptions in order to have an up-to-date handle on our self-concept. In order to better understand the self-concept, let's consider the characteristics that make up the self.

The Self Is Subjective

This means that we do not see ourselves without bias. It is difficult to step outside of ourselves and form a factual opinion of the person we are viewing. When we are engaged in an argument, we find it difficult, if not impossible, to see where we may be wrong. After all, we are inside with all those thoughts, emotions, and memories running around. We are too involved with our self to be able to clearly monitor our own behavior, to see our behavior from another point of view. We can also be biased by old perceptions of our self that are no longer true. For instance, I (Tracey) have always considered myself to be poor at math; therefore, that's the label I gave myself. A few years ago my best friend, after hearing me talk about how poor I was in math, said "Oh, really?" She continued, "Who is it that kept books for Holiday Inn; who figures out several income tax forms; who pays the bills, balances the checkbook, and figures her students' grades?" She had effectively shown me that while I might have been a poor mathematician at one time, I was no longer that person. It is important to take a periodic inventory to see if your self-concept is up to date.

Not only do we distort our own self-concept, but others can distort it as well. Simply stated, people lie to us. Their feedback can be favorable or negative, but it is distorted because it is not the truth. It can be prompted by good or bad intentions, but nonetheless it causes us to form an unrealistic self-concept and can affect our self-esteem. A professional assistant, with good intentions, may mislead his boss by constantly reinforcing her belief that she is an organized person. However, it is the assistant who sees to the details of the boss's everyday affairs. If the boss is told often enough that she is well organized, she will begin to believe it, even though it is untrue. Children who are constantly told they are poor learners by those around them will begin to think of themselves that way. Even if they have a high IQ, their grades will suffer and they will label themselves as slow. This concept is known as **self-fulfilling prophecy**. If we predict, or prophesize, something to be true, we often behave in ways to cause this prediction to become reality. A self-fulfilling prophecy can be negative or positive. Believing we can do something is just as powerful as believing we can't do something.

While it is not necessary to subscribe to the philosophy that "thinking it will make it so," belief in the outcome of an event will certainly have an effect on the result. If we think we can accomplish a task, we will, at the very least, attempt it. On the other hand, if we think we will fail, we may

 ## Activity for Further Understanding

Self-Fulfilling Prophecies

The following activity will help you more fully understand how your negative beliefs affect your self-concept.

1. List three negative self-fulfilling prophecies that you have. Begin your statement with "I can't _____ (fill in the blank).

2. Decide the following about each prophecy:

    a. What part of your self-concept is creating the prophecy? (Example: I think I'm shy, so I can't meet new people.)

    b. Was it originally self- or other-imposed? What social comparisons or reflected appraisals helped form it?

    c. Is it really "I can't," "I won't," or is it an "I don't know how"?

3. After making the decisions in #2, take some time to reflect on how these prophecies have kept you from achieving your goals, living life to its fullest, realizing your full potential, or forming successful relationships. It might be helpful to write down these ideas and list some possible ways to change these negative self-fulfilling prophecies.

4. Now rewrite the statements in #1 using the words "I won't" instead of "I can't." (You may find this somewhat painful at first, but actually it is probably closer to the truth.) There are really very few things we can't do. Accept responsibility for making things true because you believe them to be so and you will find you can change more than you believed possible.

never start the project, and we will not be able to accomplish our goal. If we build up numerous negative self-fulfilling prophecies, our self-concept will suffer. We may develop a lower self-esteem, viewing ourselves as failures. Although believing in our capabilities may not assure complete success, it will certainly enhance the outcome. Other people make predictions for us as well. For example, a mother who tells her daughter she will never be good enough to dance on Broadway may result in that child skipping dance rehearsals or engaging in other behaviors, causing the prediction to become reality.

The examples above show us how our self-concept can become distorted by others' feedback. Are you receiving any distorted feedback or holding on to an outdated view of yourself?

The Self Resists Change

People change from day to day, month to month, and year to year. Their self-concept must constantly be updated to keep pace with these changes. Yet, it is difficult to recognize and accept such change. This reluctance to accept change is a deterrent to making changes. We all have a tendency to hold on to what we know. It is comfortable, safe, and secure to do so. We are afraid to change because we don't know what might happen after the change occurs. We are fearful of the unknown. Since facing change means facing the unknown, we can see why change is so difficult.

Tracey has had a weight problem all her life. Many times over the years she has lost significant poundage and achieved a slim appearance. The scale told her one thing, but her self-concept told her the opposite. She clung to the self-image of being fat. Consequently, the weight came back and her self-concept of being fat remained. As another example of resisting change, students who return to college several years after high school often hold the same self-concept they had as high school juniors or seniors. If they were poor students then, they still consider themselves to be poor students. Even when they receive a good grade they consider it luck, or something other than their own accomplishment. If they are unsuccessful at recognizing change, they will find old habits returning and new beliefs sabotaged. In order to have positive self-esteem and a healthy up-to-date self-concept, we must attempt to change despite the fear involved. Remember, courage is not being without fear but is acting despite fear. How we perceive ourselves has a direct influence on how we communicate with others.

Communication and the Self

At the beginning of this chapter, we stated that understanding your self-concept and self-esteem is essential to effective communication. Without this knowledge, relationships can suffer. If we understand ourselves, our strengths and limitations, we can feel confident when we communicate. With a true understanding of our self comes positive self-esteem. This gives us the confidence and insight to be able to express ourselves clearly, state our beliefs forcefully, and listen to others intently. We can have positive, effective communication experiences by knowing who we are and feeling comfortable with ourselves.

The quiz in the following activity box allows you to examine your reactions and feelings in interpersonal relationships and should give you a basic idea of whether your self-concept and self-esteem are hindering your attempts at communication.

 ## Activity for Further Understanding

Communication Effectiveness Quiz

Answer the following questions by responding either A, B, or C. Try to be honest. Picture yourself in the situation stated and answer as to how you would actually react, not how you think you *should* react.

1. In regard to other people, I generally:
   a. Think well of others.
   b. Disapprove of others.
   c. About half and half.

2. In regard to what others think about me, I generally:
   a. Expect to be accepted by others.
   b. Expect to be rejected by others.
   c. About half will like me and half will not like me.

3. When I have completed a job or school-related project, I generally:
   a. Believe I have done a good job.
   b. Believe I have done less than I could have.
   c. Half the time I think I've done well, half the time I think I did poorly.

4. When I am working for another and know that he or she is watching my performance, I generally:
   a. Perform well, and I'm not afraid of others' reactions.
   b. Perform poorly, and I'm sensitive to possible negative reactions.
   c. It really depends on the situation and the observer.

5. I prefer to work for a boss, teacher, etc., who:
   a. Demands high standards of me and can be constructively critical of my work.
   b. Expects less of me and is not very critical.
   c. It varies from situation to situation.

6. When I am around people I perceive as superior to me in some way, I generally:

   a. Feel comfortable with them.

   b. Feel threatened by them.

   c. Sometimes I'm OK; sometimes I'm uncomfortable.

7. When others make negative comments about me, I generally:

   a. Can defend myself against their comments.

   b. Cannot defend myself against what they say.

   c. It's about equal.

8. In regard to others, I generally:

   a. Make up my own mind and am not much influenced by others.

   b. Find myself being frequently influenced by other's opinions and beliefs.

   c. It depends on the person attempting to influence me.

Scoring:

   3 points for every A answer

   0 points for every B answer

   1 point for every C answer

If you scored between 16 and 24, you probably have a normal self-concept with healthy, positive self-esteem. Your positive self-esteem helps you feel comfortable with other people. This leads to more disclosure and understanding. Even though you may not consider yourself to be a perfect communicator, you are usually effective when speaking with others. If you scored less than 16, chances are you are not as happy with yourself as you would like. You may need to reexamine your self-beliefs and see where old beliefs or distorted feedback from others is influencing you and your communication with others. You may be overly influenced by reflected appraisals and social comparisons. You need to understand that you could be harming yourself by continuing to believe these negative impressions. Your lower self-esteem is making your communication less effective. People will begin to view you more favorably if you allow your self-concept to change and develop more positive self-esteem.

Making Positive Changes

After examining your self-concept and how it affects your communication, you may have discovered that you would like to make some changes. If so, the following three steps can help you accomplish your goal.

- *Step One: Make change a priority.* By making change a priority in your life you will create a positive self-fulfilling prophecy, and change is more likely to occur. We are all busy people and have much to accomplish on a daily basis. If changing your self-concept is not a priority, you will find it difficult to maintain the energy and mind-set required to make the change. Since the nature of the self-concept is to resist change, making *any* change will be difficult. By making change a priority, you can eliminate distractions that prevent you from achieving your goal.

Consider all the tasks that you must accomplish each day. Include a change in self-concept on your to-do list. If you are too busy or emotionally overwhelmed to change, then don't attempt it. Once you have made the decision to postpone change, leave it alone. Constantly reminding yourself will only create a negative influence on your self-esteem, making the change more difficult later. It is, however, important to realize that the "perfect" time to make a change rarely occurs.

- *Step Two: Develop the skills to make change possible.* Changing your self-concept requires you to figure out why you haven't already made the change. Is the desired change one you believe you can't make, one you have not changed because you won't, or one that you don't know how to change? If it is truly one that you cannot change (due to physical limitations or other people involved), it is best to accept this fact and live with it. Just remember that much of what we consider impossible really can be done if we are diligent and willing to commit to whatever it takes, even if it isn't easy!

Many of our self-fulfilling prophecies are "I won't" change because it means giving up certain beliefs and behaviors that are firmly established and comfortable. For example, it is more accurate for me to say, "I won't lose weight," than to say, "I can't lose weight." I can lose; I've done so in the past. What I *won't* do is give up fast food, chocolate, and snacking between meals, and I won't make myself do a daily exercise routine! If your desired change is an "I won't," then you have to decide if the change will be more beneficial to you than the fulfillment you receive from keeping your current behavior. Remember, you are the only one who can make a change work. If you don't commit to the change and give up those activities or beliefs that reinforce what you want to change, give up trying to change until you find the motivation to do so.

Finally, if the change is one that you don't know how to make, you will need to educate yourself. There are several helpful sources available when you find you are at a loss on how to accomplish some goal. Bookstores and libraries contain numerous "self-help" and "how-to" manuals. Read books, take a course to learn the skills you need, or find a chat room devoted to your need. Observe people who display the traits you wish to develop or talk to an expert. Once you have learned a way to change and mastered the new skill, you will find that the change in your self-concept has caused your self-esteem to soar.

- *Step Three: Stick to your decision to change.* The last step to making a change in your self-concept is sticking to your decision to change. Self-concepts are not formed quickly. They are the culmination of many years of information and interpretations. It is unrealistic to believe that any change will come quickly. Having the will to stick to your decision will carry you through the times when the desired change seems slow in coming.

Changing your self-concept may require you to remove yourself from negative influences. This may mean developing new relationships or changing your environment. This is a difficult part of the process, but essential to the successful completion of your goal. Seeking and developing new skills is time-consuming and often frustrating, but well worth the investment. Twelve-step programs, such as Alcoholics Anonymous, teach people to approach change one day at a time. This practice is very useful when trying to stick to your decision for change. You only have to tackle the change one day at a time. Thinking about changing for the rest of your life is overwhelming and can cause you to give up before you ever begin. However, tackling one day at a time will help you achieve your goal. No one can face the thought of living on a low-calorie diet for the rest of their life, but most people are capable of controlling their appetite for one day at a time.

Depending on the magnitude of the change, it could take years to achieve your goal. To tackle a large goal, make smaller goals that are easier to accomplish. When you achieve a small goal be sure to reward yourself in some appropriate and positive manner. This will help you stick to your decision for long-term change. Be sure to seek out positive reinforcement from yourself and others, making it easier to persevere.

The decision of whether or not you should change is up to you. However, remember that your self-concept must be assessed and updated in order to achieve effective communication. Knowing how the self-concept is formed and influenced, its characteristics, and the effect it has on our communication will help you monitor and continually develop a positive self-concept. This will result in higher self-esteem and improved communication.

Conclusion

Your self-concept is what makes up your very essence as a human being. What you think about yourself affects not only your own life, but your communication and your relationships with others as well. You are responsible for who you think you are and how you feel about yourself. You may decide to change something about your self and only *you* can change *you*. Knowing about your self and making changes if necessary helps your overall self-concept. A positive self-concept will help you be a more effective communicator, another key to survival.

DISCUSSION QUESTIONS

1. What is the difference between self-concept and self-esteem?

2. Discuss one part of your self-concept that was influenced by an authority figure.

3. Discuss one part of your self-concept that was influenced by social comparisons.

4. Using the definition of a significant other found in this chapter, explain why the media might be a significant other in *your* life.

5. Discuss a self-fulfilling prophecy that you have experienced and trace its effect on your self-concept and self-esteem.

6. Think of one aspect about your self that you would like to change. Describe how the change would affect your self-concept and your strategy for making the change, using the three-step process discussed in this chapter.

KEY TERMS

authority figures
group
parents
peers
referent group
reflected appraisal

self-concept
self-esteem
self-fulfilling prophecy
significant others
social comparisons

chapter six

Self-Disclosure

I've got a secret . . . or two . . . or three . . .

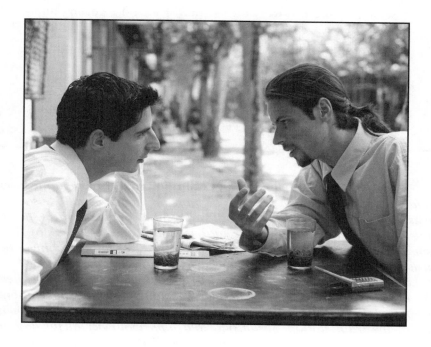

CHAPTER HIGHLIGHTS

- We are complex beings with many characteristics.
- We can let others know us by willingly revealing personal information.
- This process is called self-disclosure, and we do it for many reasons.
- We disclose to feel better, clarify our feelings, and justify our actions.
- Self-disclosing can promote reciprocity, maintain our relationships, and improve our overall health.
- Sometimes we use self-disclosure to maintain our identities, to have social control, and to manipulate others.
- If we choose not to disclose, we might lie, hint, withhold, or mask instead.
- Self-disclosure involves current, personal, and revealing information.
- Our emotional state, culture, and gender all produce challenges to self-disclosing.
- There are many elements to consider when choosing to self-disclose.
- You can become a more effective communicator by using self-disclosure.

Thank goodness they had talked about where their communication had gone astray, thought Jason as he hung up the phone with Susan. It was a simple misunderstanding that had resulted in both of them spending several hours thinking their relationship was over! He was sure that some day, they'd be able to laugh about it, but not tonight. Tonight he was relieved but exhausted. He knew Susan felt the same way. She had told him how scared she had been when she thought he hadn't waited for her at The Station. She had thought he wanted to end their relationship. He told her that he thought the same thing when she hadn't shown up at the train station. Susan had told him about her awful day at work. That explained why she had sounded the way she did on the phone. He'd told her he had a surprise and didn't want to give it away. That's why his phone call was short and sounded curt. He hadn't told her what the surprise was even now on the phone, but she had tried to get him to tell her. They'd made a date for dinner tomorrow night. This time he'd pick her up at her place so there wouldn't be any confusion. He smiled and thought about tomorrow night, and then he spotted the roses on the floor where he had dropped them. They didn't look too good. He'd get new ones tomorrow.

Susan was so happy! It was funny how you could quickly go from being depressed to being happy. A smile crossed her lips. Jason loved her. He'd told her over and over again on the phone after they'd straightened out their misunderstanding. Susan felt a little silly; how could she really have thought otherwise? She was lucky that she and Jason had always been able to talk and disclose their thoughts and feelings to each other. It was what made their relationship so fulfilling. Jason wouldn't tell her the BIG surprise that he was so excited about, even though she'd directly asked him what it was. Susan loved surprises. Jason knew this because early in their relationship they'd talked about it. She had told him tonight that she thought he was afraid to make their relationship more permanent because she wasn't making a bigger salary. She'd been pushing herself so hard at work to make more money. He'd told her that nothing could be further from the truth and then he laughed! She'd ask him why he had laughed. Did that mean he found her insecurity funny? He'd reassured her, said no, and told her she would understand tomorrow night when he picked her up. He said it was part of the surprise.

What Is Self-Disclosure?

In the previous chapter we discussed self-concept and self-esteem. We learned that who we think we are and how we feel about ourselves influences our interpersonal communication relationships. We are complex beings with many characteristics. We are often a mystery to ourselves. Think about that statement. If we don't know ourselves, what we are feeling, or why we are reacting a certain way, how difficult would it be for another person to know? We can unlock that mystery and let others know us by willingly revealing information about ourselves. This is called self-disclosure. **Self-disclosure** is the act of deliberately revealing your intimate thoughts, feelings, and experiences to another person.

There are many characteristics and experiences attached to any one person. Our many experiences create our personalities and cause us to be unique human beings. Some characteristics about us are already known by others. This common information may include where we live, whether or not we are single, where we work, if we own pets, and what kind of car we drive. This information can be obtained easily by others through observation of our daily routine. It is straightforward and verifiable information. It is generally thought of as topical or **surface information**. Although this type of information may cover a wide range of attributes, it lacks any depth. Surface information does not fall under the category of self-disclosure.

There is also information about each of us that is not commonly known to others. This information is usually very personal and intimate, and may include our fears, our goals, our dreams, our successes, our failures, our weaknesses, and our personal habits. This information cannot be found through casual observation of our daily routine. The only way this information can be known to others is if we choose to tell them. We must purposely disclose this information about ourselves. In other words, we make a deliberate decision to share personal thoughts and feelings with others. Self-disclosure is not a "slip of the tongue" or unconscious nonverbal messages. It is a deliberate act, a choice.

Self-Disclosure Is a Choice

Sometimes we make the decision to disclose personal information to others. If we decide to tell someone private information about ourselves, it is because we feel we will benefit in some way from the disclosure. Maybe we believe our relationship will grow stronger if the other person knows more about us. Maybe we believe we will feel better if we reveal a secret fear that has been haunting us and hindering our success on the job, at school, or in our personal relationships. Maybe we believe telling the truth will make us a better person because "honesty is the best policy." If we believe that there is some benefit in sharing personal information, for whatever reason, we will choose to self-disclose. We make this choice because we perceive that we will gain something; in other words, our act of self-disclosure will be beneficial. If we perceive no gain, or believe the risk is too great, we don't tell.

Sometimes we make the decision of not telling others intimate information. If we make the choice not to tell information, it is because we perceive no benefit, or worse, believe disclosing will harm us in some way. This perception is fueled by fear. We might believe that if someone knows our thoughts and feelings that person may use that information against us in the future or will hold some power over us. If someone knows everything about us, we become vulnerable. What if that person tells someone else our secret? What if the information we tell results in laughter, crying, or worse yet, anger or disappointment? Sometimes we believe it is dangerous to be honest with others. By revealing private information, we become an open book, subject to scrutiny and judgment, making it risky to reveal private information. Therefore, sensing danger and risk, we make the conscious choice not to share personal information. We don't believe revealing the truth is beneficial; the risk outweighs the benefit.

There are many reasons why we might tell someone intimate information. There are also numerous reasons we may choose not to disclose. Our life experiences, our environments, and the family lifestyle in which we grew up will all have an effect on our desire to disclose. Negative experiences with past disclosures may result in our being fearful of self-disclosure. If we've been hurt or embarrassed, we aren't inclined to put ourselves in that type of situation again.

We all have a past and none of us are perfect. We think that disclosure of our indiscretions might result in an unfavorable perception or project a negative public image. This is a reasonable belief. Self-disclosure is not an endorsement for unconditional openness. It doesn't require us to share everything about ourselves with everyone we meet. Remember, it is not always necessary to disclose past experiences and beliefs. In fact, there are some disclosures that might hinder rather than help communication. Disclosing may lead others to misjudge us or bring unnecessary complications to the situation. If the information isn't directly related to why we feel the way we do now, it can remain undisclosed. On the other hand, if there is a past experience that has direct bearing on why we feel or think a certain way, it may need to be disclosed. Disclosure may be necessary in order for another person to understand us completely.

Why Self-Disclose?

Why would you want to share your thoughts and feelings with another person? Since there are obviously risks involved with sharing personal data, why might you choose to self-disclose? What is the purpose of self-disclosure? There are several reasons why we share information about ourselves, and the results of our disclosures can be very positive!

- *To Feel Better.* Sometimes we feel the need to talk in order to feel better. We might discuss our fear of failure on a new job or our fear of failing our classes. We might feel uncomfortable in the role of new parent or be unsure about ourselves in a relationship or situation. We often talk to someone else as a way to clear the air and "get it off our chest." This reason for self-disclosure is known as **self-catharsis**. We often feel better physically and mentally after sharing information. It is as if a tremendous weight has been lifted from us. We see blue skies where there once was gray. This is a very rewarding reason for disclosing if the purpose of our disclosure is to help the other person empathize with us. Self-catharsis shouldn't be used to get even or clear our conscience.

- *To Clarify Our Feelings.* We often feel the need to share in order to clarify our ideas and feelings. We use others as a sounding board. By expressing our dreams or desires to someone else, we often paint a clearer picture of them in our own mind. When we find ourselves confused about something, it frequently helps to discuss our thoughts and feelings with others to get their feedback. In this fash-

ion we use other people as catalysts to help make sense of our
internal thoughts. This form of self-disclosure is called **self-clarification**, due to its ability to help us see ourselves with more clarity.

- ***To Validate Our Actions.*** Sometimes we disclose to others as a
way to justify our own actions. We will tell them information about
ourselves because we want them to validate it. Think of a parking
garage where the attendant hands you a parking ticket. You can
park for free if you prove you were at the mall by having one of the
shops inside "validate" or stamp your ticket. We disclose information for much the same reason. When we disclose our feelings,
thoughts, or dreams to another person and that person positively
reinforces what we say, we feel like our ticket has been stamped. We
have been proven right or validated. In the process of seeking others' opinions to confirm that what we think or do is appropriate,
we often make our feelings clearer to ourselves. This is called **self-
validation** and is closely related to the idea of self-clarification
because our thoughts and feelings become clearer to us while we
are proving them to others. Remember that self-disclosing for this
reason carries the risk of finding out that others don't agree with
your action or decision. If we are merely seeking a positive
response, like, "You are right, that's perfect," and become defensive
if someone doesn't respond the way we wanted, we are actually
using self-disclosure to manipulate, which we'll discuss later.

- ***To Promote Reciprocity.*** We might decide to disclose information
to another in the hope she might self-disclose, also. We hope that if
this individual sees that we are not afraid to tell the truth about
something we did or how we feel, the door will be open for her to
tell us honest information. Through self-disclosing, we show this
person that we trust her with our intimate thoughts, thereby inviting her to respond in kind. This exchange process is known as **reciprocity**. Most people can identify with the concept of "you scratch
my back and I'll scratch yours." Reciprocity, as a reason for self-disclosure, follows this same mind-set. If you reveal information of an
intimate nature, another might be encouraged to follow suit. You
have shown you believe it is beneficial to reveal honest information
about your feelings and opinions. You have shown the person that
you trust her. This courage might instill in her the courage to self-
disclose, too. Reciprocity enhances relationships of all kinds—
romantic, platonic, familial, and professional.

- ***To Maintain Relationships.*** Sharing our intimate thoughts and
feelings by self-disclosing can help relationships grow. Relationships can become healthier when we are honest and truthful with
one another. Honesty leads to trust, and mutual trust deepens our
interpersonal relationships. Reciprocity, through self-disclosure,

results in validation that the relationship is honest and important to both parties. Numerous research studies indicate that couples who self-disclose remain together far longer than those who don't. It is easier to understand someone, and be close to him, when there are few secrets or hidden elements. It is healthy to engage in self-disclosure, as it is significantly effective for relationship maintenance.

- *To Improve Our Health.* Our personal health improves when we share our emotions. Studies have shown that when we suppress our emotions by keeping our feelings bottled up inside of us, we cause our stress levels to increase. Stress goes to work on our immune system causing hypertension, headaches, backaches, ulcers, and other physical problems. Many health problems have been directly linked to people who "close" themselves off to others. If we disclose information, and don't keep our thoughts and feelings bottled up inside, it can be beneficial to our mental and physical health. We can prevent problems linked to nondisclosure. Therefore self-disclosure serves as a way to maintain our health.

- *To Maintain Our Identities.* In the previous chapter we learned about our public and private selves. We discussed how we might present one personality to our friends and a different one to our grandparents. This is called **identity management**. What we disclose and to whom is a significant factor in presenting an appropriate public self for each situation we are in. Therefore, when and what you disclose can help you manage your own identity. Note that we aren't talking about lying or creating a "false" persona for the purposes of manipulating other people; we are talking about appropriate self-management.

- *To Have Social Control.* When we are trying to be on our "best behavior" and present an appropriate public self in a social situation, we attempt to control the perceptions of others. This element is closely related to identity management and is known as **social control**. We disclose information we think promotes our strengths and choose not to disclose information that we believe makes us a liability. For example, let's say you are meeting with the CEO of your company prior to a decision about a possible promotion. It is widely known among company employees that the CEO is very conservative, traditional, and a devout Catholic. During your interview you might disclose views that are similar in nature, making sure your tattoo doesn't show! Again, we want to stress that we aren't talking about projecting a false personality just to help you land the job. We're talking about making a choice about the depth and breadth of the topics disclosed.

- *To Manipulate Others.* We also use self-disclosure for the purpose of deliberately achieving a specific result. When we choose to disclose with the sole purpose of getting someone to react a particular way, we are using self-disclosure to manipulate the situation. Unlike social control, where we are "putting our best foot forward," manipulation is inappropriate. In fact it could be argued that since self-disclosure requires honesty, manipulation doesn't even classify as real self-disclosure. We needn't engage in a lengthy argument to understand that disclosure or not, people often use their thoughts and feelings for the purpose of "getting what they want." Manipulation is difficult to recognize because it is often disguised as another form of disclosure. For instance, it may seem like self-validation or social control when it is really an attempt to achieve personal reward. In fact, we sometimes justify using manipulation by telling ourselves (and others) that we were only trying to be on our "best behavior."

Your authors feel it is important to include manipulation as a use of self-disclosure for several reasons. First, you need to recognize manipulation when you see it (in yourself and others) and learn to react appropriately. Second, manipulation is a significant factor in promoting defensiveness, which will be discussed in detail in chap-

 ## Activity for Further Understanding

Self-Disclosure Assignment

For three days keep track of your dominant emotions. For each situation do the following:

1. Describe the situation. Who was involved? What happened or what was being discussed?

2. What was your emotional response? Be sure to include all the feelings you were aware of during, and as a result of, this encounter.

3. Did you disclose these emotions to another person? If so, what did you say and do? Be sure to include your verbal and nonverbal communication. If you didn't disclose, what was your reason for not sharing?

4. What was the outcome of your disclosure or nondisclosure? How effective or ineffective were you?

5. After three days, you will have numerous situations to examine. You will not necessarily have included every emotion you experienced during those three days. However, you should have a database from which you can draw some observations. Analyze this data.

   a. Do you tend to disclose emotions or repress them?

   b. Are you usually effective in taking responsibility for what you are feeling?

   c. What happens when you choose not to disclose?

   d. In general, what have you learned about your own self-disclosure?

ter 9. For now, it is important to understand that using disclosure for this purpose is not effective communication. In the short term it may appear to create benefits, but eventually it causes total break-down in communication.

Self-disclosure has many uses as we've just discussed. Most of these uses are positive and increase effective communication between people. However, when self-disclosure is used to manipulate others, it ultimately leads to ineffective communication. In general, we should engage in self-disclosure as much as possible in our interpersonal relationships. The benefits of doing so outweigh the risks. What we perceive as risk is really fear that can be overcome. Self-disclosing can impact us and others positively and help us maintain good relationships.

When We Choose Not to Self-Disclose

There are times when we choose not to self-disclose. What happens when we are with a person we don't trust who is expecting us to talk about ourselves and our reactions? What about those situations where we are too fearful to disclose? In these cases, when we feel pressured to self-disclose but have determined that the risk is far greater than any benefit, we might decide to engage in behaviors that mimic self-disclosure but are actually not disclosure at all.

- **We may lie.** Most of us have lied at one time or another. Whether or not you believe lying is morally or ethically correct is not really the issue here. Relevant to our discussion of self-disclosure is the idea that most of us believe there is some benefit to lying on occasion. We believe small lies are, for the most part, harmless ways of avoiding possible conflict. We often tell untrue information in an effort to please others, or at least that's what we think we are doing. If we speak about ourselves when pressured to, even if the information is untrue, then we have fulfilled the expectations of the other person to share or respond to her. We look good, and ultimately we believe we have fulfilled our obligation. Thus, having gained some information about us, the other person seems to feel good too. We have lied, but justify doing so because we do not want others to think badly of us, which might happen if they know the real truth. We may even lie because we don't want them to be upset with us for not wanting to share information with them. Perhaps we are afraid of the truth, for whatever reason, and lying appears safer than refusing to disclose any information at all. We may lie because we believe if we don't say *something*, we will make the person feel guilty or cause him to be upset.

If we choose to lie we have not successfully engaged in self-disclo-sure. In fact, we have purposefully led another person to believe something that will influence her in future interactions with us. This can cause further misunderstandings. The definition and char-acteristics of self-disclosure state that information revealed must be true and honest. It is this information that ultimately will allow us to be known by others. Lying does not accomplish this task. Lying is not an acceptable alternative to disclosing.

- *We may hint.* When we feel caught in a situation where the other person is demanding disclosure from us, we may choose to be vague or hint at what we think or feel. We believe for some reason that disclosing is too risky, but since the situation demands a response we may choose one that does not use direct or specific language, so we aren't "pinned down." If the other person inter-prets our reaction in a negative way, we can feel justified by saying it was a misunderstanding. Hinting often involves displaying thoughts and feelings with nonverbal behaviors rather than verbal opinions. We may frown, avoid eye contact, or raise the volume of our voice rather than say we don't agree, feel ashamed, or think we are being ignored. It is likely that when we choose to hint, rather than to be direct, we are manipulating the situation or person involved. We've already established that this behavior is detrimental to effective communication in the long run. Hinting is not an acceptable alternative to self-disclosure either.

- *We may withhold or mask.* There are times when we feel pres-sured to disclose but we choose to withhold or mask our reactions. We keep our thoughts and feelings "inside" by carefully controlling our verbal and nonverbal reactions. People choose this alternative to self-disclosure for a variety of personal reasons, including nega-tive experiences with self-disclosure in the past. Some believe that withholding or masking is a better moral choice than lying. Many people engage in these behaviors because they are trying to protect the other person from being hurt. People who choose to mask or withhold their feelings are often perceived as being "cold." In fact, about the only situation this behavior is appropriate for in our cul-ture is when we are playing poker! These behaviors are not accept-able alternatives either.

Characteristics of Self-Disclosure

Self-disclosure allows people to get to know one another on a deeper level. It allows others to share in your goals, dreams, fears, and failures. It allows others to know our feelings, ideas, and expectations. It enhances relationships and promotes effective communication. Although it deals with numerous aspects, self-disclosure has some key characteristics.

- *Current, Personal, and Revealing.* Self-disclosure involves personal and revealing information about ourselves. That means that the information is not commonly known, nor can it be found through casual observation or conversation. This data includes our current thoughts and feelings, not the fact that we were angry last Tuesday. We can't do anything about the past because it is over. We can't change it no matter how much we want to. Sometimes we need to share past experiences to help empathize with another person, but when self-disclosing it isn't necessary to share our life history. In fact, disclosure of unrelated material may result in ineffective communication. Past experiences need be disclosed only when they have a direct effect on the present situation. Information can only be classified as self-disclosure when it is uncommon information told by us, about us, intentionally to another person, usually as it occurs in the present.

- *Truthful and Honest.* The information we reveal must be true and honest. In other words, to self-disclose we must tell our partner what we really believe has occurred. Furthermore, we must explain our reactions and feelings about what we are sharing. If we don't, it may result in others making false assumptions, or force them to be mind readers. The only way for anyone to really know what someone else is thinking and feeling is through self-disclosure. When we fail to express how we are feeling, we force others to interpret our thoughts and actions. Their perception may be very different from what we are truly experiencing. Honesty and truthfulness are essential components to self-disclosure.

- *Mutual and Confidential.* Remember, self-disclosure is a deliberate choice. When we disclose to a particular person we believe the information should go no further. Therefore, both parties must have a mutual understanding that the information being shared is personal and intimate, and should not be shared.

- *Dyadic and Continual.* Not surprisingly, research verifies that most self-disclosure takes place between two people (a dyad) and over a period of time. It also occurs in relationships that are perceived as being mutually agreeable. Your own experiences probably match the research. Typically, we disclose to only one person at a time as our relationship with that person grows and deepens (a result of effective disclosure). While there are instances where a stranger may disclose and we may reciprocate, these only occur during brief temporary conditions. Most of these encounters are for reasons of self-catharsis, self-clarification, or self-validation. Indeed the reason they occur at all is the fact that we and the stranger don't anticipate ever seeing each other again! Since we have no past or future relationship with this person the risk of self-disclosing is relatively low. In reality, most disclosure involves those we trust and have known over a long period of time.

As you may have concluded, there are many opportunities for disclosing our thoughts and feelings. Yet in considering the characteristics of self-disclosure, you can see that disclosures at the ultimate level are relatively scarce. Disclosure usually takes place in positive relationships, in which we perceive little risk, and that give us the opportunity to strengthen our relationship. Making the choice to self-disclose isn't simple and shouldn't be taken lightly. There are real challenges in making that choice. That's where we'll focus next.

Challenges to Self-Disclosure

Making an appropriate decision to self-disclose in any given situation is difficult. Trust is the major issue. Can I trust this person not to share my disclosure? Fear is also an issue. Will he reject me if I tell him what I think? As we've suggested throughout this chapter, self-disclosure is risky and we don't suggest that you should practice it without being aware of the many difficulties and possible outcomes. Deciding to self-disclose can have a major effect (positive or negative) upon our personal and professional relationships. Considering the following challenges before you disclose can help you be a more effective communicator.

Emotional Challenges

Our thoughts and our feelings are often reactions to situations. We may think someone is being unfair to us. We may feel disappointed, resentful, or angry. When we self-disclose it is effective to disclose both our thoughts and our feelings. Yet this can present a challenge for a variety of reasons.

When we disclose, we often say things like, "I feel like you don't trust me." Such a disclosure represents a thought or opinion, based on an emotion, such as feeling rejected. This can cause problems if we don't explain why we feel the way we do, or explain the source of our feelings: "I feel like you don't trust me because . . . ." If the other person is aware of only our emotional response and continues her behavior, we conclude she intends to "hurt" us. The fact is, we really haven't been truthful and honest about our feelings and how her actions have contributed to them.

Another challenge is with our "feelings vocabulary." We typically don't express feelings with much clarity; in fact sometimes we aren't even aware of what we are feeling! We are often confused! It's impossible to self-disclose effectively if we aren't clear. Remember, the person you are disclosing to must understand your thoughts and feelings for your disclosure to be effective.

Cultural Challenges

Our culture is frequently responsible for guiding how we communicate. We tend to learn from the behavior of those around us. Since we are now interconnected globally and many of us live in or travel to multiculturally diverse communities, it is common for the average person to be exposed to people of other cultures. While it isn't the intent of this text to make you aware of all the various differences in cultural disclosure (we're not even sure that's possible), we do want you to remember that there are vast differences between what Americans believe is appropriate disclosure and what members of other societies accept as appropriate disclosure.

U.S. citizens tend to disclose more openly, more frequently, and about more topics than citizens of Great Britain, Puerto Rico, Japan, China, and most Middle Eastern countries. For example, in the United States we often discuss our family with our coworkers. We share stories about our children or the family vacation; colleagues in Japan would consider this to be inappropriate. In Mexico there is a strong cultural emphasis on disclosing positive information but withholding negative information. Negative information is only disclosed to intimate friends or family and only after a long time has passed. In the U.S. we typically disclose information about situations to someone we trust rather quickly, whether the information is negative or positive.

Adding gender to cultural aspects shows us that men in the United States tend to disclose more frequently than men in other cultures. This disclosure is often viewed by masculine dominated cultures as a sign of weakness on the part of U.S. males.

There are too many cultural differences related to disclosing to discuss here, but we believe that you need to be aware of their existence when faced with an intercultural personal or professional relationship.

Gender Challenges

Gender plays a significant role in self-disclosure as well. It probably won't surprise you to know that universally men self-disclose less than women. In the next chapter we'll discover some reasons why this is true. Our purpose here is to point out the different ways that men and women in the United States use and react to self-disclosure. These differences can lead to communication breakdowns that may end in an argument. Consider the following:

- Women increase self-disclosures as intimacy grows.
- Men will self-disclose more in the initial phases of a relationship.

- Men tend to reach a comfort level with self-disclosure and maintain it, even when the relationship has grown intimate.
- Men have more topics they won't share with women.
- Women self-disclose to friends and extended family more often then men.
- Women are more likely than men to avoid self-disclosure when there is a perception of possible emotional pain to themselves or others.
- Men are more likely to avoid self-disclosure to maintain control (if I don't tell you, you can't use it against me).

Gender differences can cause misunderstandings when it comes to self-disclosure, but the good news is that regardless of gender, when reciprocal disclosure occurs, relationships deepen.

Guidelines for Self-Disclosure

By now you probably understand that effective use of self-disclosure is an essential survival skill in the pursuit of rewarding communication. If you believe this is a skill you'd like to sharpen, you might find that your answers to the questions below serve as helpful guidelines for self-disclosing. The more you practice disclosing personal information, the more skillful you'll become.

Should I Self-Disclose?

- You need to consider if self-disclosing is appropriate. Is it the best behavior in this situation and under these circumstances?
- You need to decide if the topic of your self-disclosure is appropriate. Remember that your interpretation of what is appropriate may not be the same as someone else's. Consider the recipient of your self-disclosure when making the choice to disclose. Self-disclosure about such topics as your HIV status, your income, or your spiritual beliefs may seem appropriate to you but not to someone else.
- Make sure your motivation for self-disclosing is to help create or promote mutual understanding, not to get revenge or manipulate another person.
- Evaluate the risk factor in self-disclosing. Sometimes disclosure might be unnecessary and could actually make things worse. If your spouse is crabby due to lack of sleep, it probably isn't necessary to disclose your reactions to her crabbiness. It would be more effective to empathize about her lack of sleep. And, of course, self-disclosure should never put you in danger.

When and How Should I Self-Disclose?

- Choose to self-disclose in relationships that have existed over a period of time.

- Start your self-disclosure gradually, moving from casual disclosures to more intimate ones and continue the intimate disclosure only if the other person reciprocates.

- A calm, stress-free environment is the proper setting for an intimate conversation.

   Plan a time when both you and the other person can talk. Meeting for coffee or taking a quiet walk in the park often facilitates talking.

   Minimize distractions or meet when both parties have an adequate amount of time.

   Take into consideration the other person's mood. There are times when you must wait to talk until both of you are in the mood. If your roommate just broke up with his girlfriend, it is probably not the best time to disclose how upset you are with him that he is not doing his share of the housework.

- Describe your feelings verbally. Choose the appropriate words. Be precise and clear. Contrary to what many people believe, more words don't always result in more effective communication. You should include all of the information necessary for the other person to get a clear picture or representation in his mind that matches the one in yours (refer to the discussion of the communication process in chapter 1). This will help you come as close as you can to mutual understanding.

- Learn to describe your feelings and emotions accurately. We may feel guilty and then become angry. Often we only disclose the anger (or reveal it nonverbally). It is essential in disclosure to include all the emotions we are experiencing, such as guilt and anger, and their relationship to each other and the situation.

- Accept your emotions and opinions as your own. Do not blame others for your feelings. You are in control of and responsible for your reactions, yet you can easily make the mistake of blaming others for your feelings. For example, you might say, "You make me so mad," "You drive me crazy," or "He is causing me to have a bad day." Recognize that you have a choice in how another's behavior affects you, and the effect doesn't have to be beyond your control.

How Can I Get Others to Self-Disclose?

- Be aware and open to the fact that a person's innermost feelings may involve issues that are volatile or controversial.

- Allow others to share their ideas. If you make their ideas and feelings seem wanted by listening carefully to them, you are *facilitating disclosure* and thereby working toward a healthier relationship.

- Be flexible; don't be judgmental. Remember that what the person is telling you is her opinion or feeling, coming from her own unique experience.

- Be careful not to label emotions as "good" or "bad."

- You don't have to agree, but you should try to be supportive and empathetic in your role as listener.

- Keep the disclosure confidential, even if you're not specifically asked to do so. Breaching confidentiality can result in complications and decrease trust, causing the relationship to suffer. If you know that you are likely to share information with another person like your spouse or good friend, let the person speaking know in advance or ask the discloser if you can share the information. If the person says no, then don't share it with others.

Five Steps to Effective Self-Disclosure

While there are many kinds of messages that are revealed when we self-disclose, there is a specific technique that can be used when we are trying to achieve mutual understanding. This technique consists of five steps designed to create an *effective message*. This helps ensure that our self-disclosures are clearly understood:

- *Step One: What happened?* First, you must tell the other person what you saw happen. You saw him yawn when you suggested a visit to your mom's house. She frowned when you suggested a birthday gift for your friend. He brushed by and entered the elevator first. Something occurred: this is the sense data, the raw material upon which you are basing your reaction, but it is not your actual reaction. That is step two.

- *Step Two: What does it mean?* Next you must offer your interpretation of that action. This is how things seemed from your point of view, your perception. What does the action mean to you? Why do you think the person acted that way? Was he tired or did the yawn mean he didn't want to visit Mom? Tell him what you thought the sense data meant. Be sure to use "I language" not "You language." "I thought that meant," "it seems to me," "I think that means," are all effective ways to take responsibility for your interpretation.

- *Step Three: How do you feel about it?* How does your interpretation of the action make you feel? Be very specific in your choice of words. Are you disappointed, happy, frustrated, excited, or maybe several of these? Tell the other person exactly. Remember, he didn't make you feel this way; it was your interpretation, so take responsibility for your feelings. Say, "I feel disappointed," not "You disappointed me." It's not only more honest, but less defense producing as well. Also make sure that you are expressing an emotion and not a thought. If I am at a party and tell my companion, "I feel like going home now," I am expressing a thought, not a feeling (even though I used the word "feel"). The feeling I am experiencing that has resulted in my wanting to go home may be embarrassment, fatigue, guilt, satisfaction, or a range of other feelings. State specifically what the emotion is; don't be vague by saying the word "feeling." Make sure you are direct and complete in revealing your emotions. Tell the other person all of your feelings. If one feeling led to another, share both of the emotions so that your friend will be better equipped to understand you. If you tell me you are angry, I may not understand why. If you tell me you are angry because you are disappointed in my behavior, I can better understand the anger.

- **Step Four: *What is the result?*** What are the consequences of your interpretation and emotional response? What else does the other person need to know in order to understand you? Does she need to know you need personal space or time? Do you think you should talk more? If this action were repeated, what might the outcome be? You may believe the result is obvious, but people aren't mind readers. Tell the other person your intentions based upon what you think and feel. The person may be surprised at what you think you should do. He may even think you shouldn't feel this way, but he will know why and how you are interpreting that event. You can then discuss the results mutually.

- **Step Five: *Ask for feedback.*** Remember that none of us shares exactly the same personal environment. We all perceive things a little (sometimes a lot) differently, making it necessary for us to ask for clarification. Ask if your interpretation is correct. Ask if she understands what you have said. Ask for her agreement. This is how you verify that you have sent a clear effective message.

Using the above five-step technique does not require you to take the stage and speak for half an hour. You can cover all five steps in a few sentences. Then listen to the other person's feedback. Clarify any ambiguity or misunderstandings. Keep your message unthreatening and nondefensive. We don't suggest you use this method every time you have a conversation, but it is very effective in self-disclosure that involves emotions and sensitive personal feelings.

Activity for Further Understanding

Effective Message

Write an effective five-step message for the following situations. Keep it short but complete.

1. Your child (either sex) is 16. He or she has decided that it is no longer necessary to have a curfew. You try to keep a tight rein on your children but believe it is time the child takes some responsibility. How will you express this to him or her?

2. You are a supervisor at work. A worker in your department has been caught stealing. Your relationship with this person is fairly close; you have a good working relationship and have occasionally enjoyed social occasions together. He needs support, but you feel he has betrayed you. What will you say when he comes to you?

3. Your partner wants to buy a handgun to keep at home for protection. You are scared your five-year-old might find it, an action that could have devastating results. How will you express your fear?

4. Your partner is an alcoholic and confesses that she needs counseling. Money is tight and you suspect that the alcoholism is merely an escape mechanism. You think the drinking is to avoid responsibility. How will you share your feelings of frustration without destroying your partner's good intentions to get help?

5. You have a teacher whom you suspect doesn't like you. You think he is deliberately humiliating you in class. You have heard that he is a very proud person, particularly where teaching and students are concerned. How can you share your feelings of helplessness so that both your egos remain intact?

Conclusion

We can let others know us better by self-disclosing—revealing intimate information about ourselves and/or about how we feel about something. These revelations can strengthen our relationships with others. Disclosing our thoughts and emotions can alert those around us to what we are thinking and feeling. Many of us fear opening up this way, but the benefits usually outweigh the losses. When we choose to share, we facilitate reciprocity in others. This leads to mutual trust and improved relationships. Self-disclosure is a vital element and one of the keys to survival.

DISCUSSION QUESTIONS

1. Name the characteristics of true self-disclosure. How often do you think you really self-disclose?

2. What are some of the benefits and some of the risks of disclosing personal information to others?

3. When might we choose to lie instead of self-disclosing? Do you believe there are times when lies are justified? Support your opinion.

4. Think of a time when you told someone your innermost thoughts. Describe the way you felt afterwards. Identify the reasons you self-disclosed, using those found in this chapter.

5. How might you set up a "proper" environment for facilitating self-disclosure?

KEY TERMS

identity management
reciprocity
self-catharsis
self-clarification

self-disclosure
self-validation
social control
surface information

Gender Communication

He Said, She Said

CHAPTER HIGHLIGHTS

- Men and women communicate and behave very differently.

- The way that they communicate with one another is called gender communication.

- The nature argument cites research that supports that these differences are due to biology.

- Biological differences are attributed to hormones and chemicals in the brain.

- The nurture argument cites research that supports that these differences are due to societal influences.

- Societal influences include environment and the media.

- Cross-communication occurs when these differences cause men and women to interpret messages the opposite way in which they were intended.

- Instead of applying the Golden Rule and treating others the way we wish to be treated, apply the opaque rule and treat others how they wish to be treated.

- The opaque rule, when applied to gender communication, can eliminate cross-communication.

- There are some quick communication tips to help men communicate more effectively with women and women to communicate more effectively with men.

- Awareness of gender differences can help you to become a more effective communicator.

Three months have elapsed since the misunderstanding about where they were to meet, and Jason and Susan can now laugh about how silly it all was. It had all turned out okay. They had moved into the company condo about a month ago and were planning a fall wedding. Tonight was Friday, the night they stay at home and watch videos. Susan is very happy with the move, and she's recently been offered a better job. Her happiness is dimmed somewhat because Jason seems distracted and preoccupied. Susan senses something is bothering Jason. She decides to put aside her "happy mood" tonight to show Jason how much she cares about him.

She brings him a Coke and says, "What's wrong?" Jason asks her to repeat what she said (he wasn't listening) and she does. He says, "Nothing" (in that tone that implies something)! Susan sits down next to him on the couch and asks, "Do you want to talk?"

"No," he says, and he gets up and moves to the recliner, leaving her sitting alone on the couch. As Jason plugs a game into the game console

and picks up the controller, Susan watches and thinks about how he said "Nothing" and the way he is acting. Obviously, "something" is bothering him. Susan knows that when she has a problem she wants Jason to listen to her talk about it to show her that he cares. Susan puts on her concerned look, walks over to the recliner and sits on the arm. "Honey, you know you can talk to me. I know something is bothering you and I want to help."

Jason, who is mentally trying to work out a problem he's having at work, says, "Did you say something?" While Susan had immediately picked up on Jason's mood and sensed he was distracted; Jason behaves as though he's barely aware of Susan's presence. In fact, to him, she was like an annoying fly buzzing around.

"Jason," she said, standing between him and the TV screen, "I said I'll listen if you want to talk." Jason wonders why she won't leave him alone. He just wants to relax and play a mindless game so he can figure out what he is going to do at work. He finds himself running through what he said to Susan in his mind. He had been very direct; he had said he didn't want to talk, so he can't figure out why she doesn't trust him to work this out alone. Susan, wanting to show how much she loves him, repeats, "Can I help?" Jason looks up and says, "I'm going to go out for a little while."

Susan is confused and disappointed. She was only trying to help. She cares about him so much. He left when they had planned to spend the evening at home together. Why did he leave her? Will he come back? Should she start calling his friends or go look for him? Jason, on the other hand, is oblivious to Susan's concerns. He has gone to the gym to work out. He left, not because he doesn't love Susan, but because he has to think some things out that have absolutely nothing to do with her. He thinks she should certainly understand work-related stress. So far he'd made it to associate, but he wanted to climb higher on the corporate ladder, and there was a very important meeting on Monday. He just needed some time to think about his presentation. Susan was interfering by interrupting his thoughts, so he decided to leave. He'd work out while he solved his problem and then go home to watch that movie. As he opened the door to the locker room he realized that he was a little miffed that Susan hadn't seemed to trust him to handle his problem without her help.

What Is Gender Communication?

Often we have heard it said that men and women are from different planets, and we're sure that Jason and Susan would agree with this statement. It often seems to them that they are trying to communicate with some alien who doesn't speak English. Actually this is a very good way of thinking about how men and women communicate. If you met someone from a different planet, how would you communicate? You'd have to learn each other's language, which wouldn't be an easy task. Then, once you were able to use each other's language, you would still need to be aware that what was said could easily be misinterpreted. As long as you were aware of this fact, you would try to use language that both of you could understand. You'd find it necessary to check the alien's interpretation of what you were saying and check it often. This analogy is exactly the way we should handle **gender communication**. Just because men and women use the same language it doesn't mean they have the same meanings for the words they use.

Before we begin our study of gender communication, it is important that you know what the information in this chapter is *not*. It is not intended to be an attempt to desex the English language by suggesting we should use the word humankind instead of mankind, or chairperson rather than chairman. It is not a political statement about sexist language or how such language may affect people's perceptions. It is not an attempt to cause conflict by insinuating that one gender communicates more effectively than the other. It is not an attempt to get men to communicate like women or women to communicate like men. The information in this chapter *is* an attempt to help you understand how and why men and women communicate differently. It will help you more accurately perceive what is being said when you communicate with others who are not the same gender as you. It will help you decrease conflict and arguments in your life. It will help you communicate more effectively with members of the opposite gender, whether they are your parent, child, employer, teacher, platonic friend, or romantic partner.

The information contained in this chapter is based on numerous research studies. In other words, what we will share with you is based on findings that have been consistently true. As in any behavior that involves

 ## Activity for Further Understanding

You Think You Know Men and Women?

The following is a quiz on gender communication styles. Put a T if you think the answer is true or an F if you think the answer is false.

_____ 1. Women talk more than men in public.

_____ 2. Men interrupt conversations more than women.

_____ 3. Women are more attentive listeners than men.

_____ 4. A man uses more direct language than a woman.

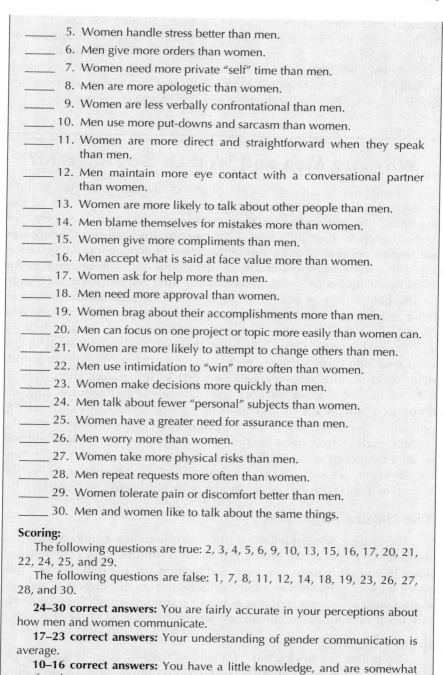

_____ 5. Women handle stress better than men.

_____ 6. Men give more orders than women.

_____ 7. Women need more private "self" time than men.

_____ 8. Men are more apologetic than women.

_____ 9. Women are less verbally confrontational than men.

_____ 10. Men use more put-downs and sarcasm than women.

_____ 11. Women are more direct and straightforward when they speak than men.

_____ 12. Men maintain more eye contact with a conversational partner than women.

_____ 13. Women are more likely to talk about other people than men.

_____ 14. Men blame themselves for mistakes more than women.

_____ 15. Women give more compliments than men.

_____ 16. Men accept what is said at face value more than women.

_____ 17. Women ask for help more than men.

_____ 18. Men need more approval than women.

_____ 19. Women brag about their accomplishments more than men.

_____ 20. Men can focus on one project or topic more easily than women can.

_____ 21. Women are more likely to attempt to change others than men.

_____ 22. Men use intimidation to "win" more often than women.

_____ 23. Women make decisions more quickly than men.

_____ 24. Men talk about fewer "personal" subjects than women.

_____ 25. Women have a greater need for assurance than men.

_____ 26. Men worry more than women.

_____ 27. Women take more physical risks than men.

_____ 28. Men repeat requests more often than women.

_____ 29. Women tolerate pain or discomfort better than men.

_____ 30. Men and women like to talk about the same things.

Scoring:

The following questions are true: 2, 3, 4, 5, 6, 9, 10, 13, 15, 16, 17, 20, 21, 22, 24, 25, and 29.

The following questions are false: 1, 7, 8, 11, 12, 14, 18, 19, 23, 26, 27, 28, and 30.

24–30 correct answers: You are fairly accurate in your perceptions about how men and women communicate.

17–23 correct answers: Your understanding of gender communication is average.

10–16 correct answers: You have a little knowledge, and are somewhat confused.

0–9 correct answers: Have you been paying attention?

human beings, there never can be an absolute. All men will not "fit" into the male behavior patterns we define, nor will all women think and act the way we say women do. Men and women are individuals and are the products of many influences, as we learned in chapter 1. However, research supports that the behaviors and the ways of thinking that we label *male* or *female* are typically true for the majority of men and women.

Why Are Men and Women So Different?

Are men and women different because of biology or because of environmental influences? There is evidence to support both sides of this argument. The *nature* supporters point to brain functions and hormones as the main reason for differences. The *nurture* supporters say differences are formed because of societal reinforcement of gender-specific behavior. Just a few years ago this was a hotly debated topic, with researchers for the nurture argument pointing to elements such as gender-specific toys to be the culprits for gender difference. More recently, advancements in brain imaging and other scientific research have tipped the scales in favor of nature. Although cultural training and nurturing matter, biology appears to be much more influential than we had previously realized. Even with this continuing research, we, your authors, believe that both nature and nurture are responsible for gender differences; more specifically we believe that we are born with physiological differences that are influenced, enhanced, or repressed by societal factors. Actually, for the purpose of learning how to be a more effective communicator, it really doesn't matter what causes the differences. We can all agree that men and women frequently fail to understand each other. Why, doesn't really matter. However, we will give you an overview of both arguments, in the hope that it will help you understand gender situations a little better.

The Nature Argument

There are a huge number of physical differences between men and women. Researchers are constantly discovering new DNA evidence and other biological reasons why men and women are different. For our purposes we will concentrate on three physical factors that appear to account for the most significant differences in our communication. They are *brain functions*, *hormones*, and *brain chemicals*.

Brain Functions

Our brains are divided into two hemispheres or sides. In general, the right side of our brain controls abstract, emotional, and creative functions, as well as the left side of our body. The left side of our brain controls detailed, practical, and concrete functions, as well as the right side of our body. The two hemispheres are connected by a bundle of nerve fibers called the **corpus callosum**. It is the corpus callosum that allows messages to travel from one side of the brain to the other. Science has found that while all of this is true for both men and women, the actual organization of the brain differs significantly in the two sexes. In women, the division between the left and right sides of the brain is more diffused, meaning some functions or abilities reside in both sides of the brain. Men's brains are more specialized. They usually use one side of their brain at a time to perform tasks. In addition, women have 25 percent more nerves connecting their two hemispheres, which allows more information to be exchanged between the left and right sides of the female brain than the male brain.

Okay, so what does all this mean with regard to communication between the sexes? Let's start by looking at emotions. It's no secret that men and women show, express, and respond differently to emotions. This behavioral difference often results in conflict. Men are accused of being less emotional, while women are blamed for being too emotional. Could the difference in the layout of our brains be responsible? Many scientists say yes. A man's center for emotion is in the right side of his brain. His centers for speech, language, and vocabulary are in the left side and are separated into two parts, one in the front and one in the back of his left brain. Since men have 25 percent fewer corpus callosum fibers connecting the right and left brain, there is *less* flow of information from side to side. Since the emotional response must cross from the right to the left to reach the verbal center of a man's brain, it is 25 percent less likely to happen. It is simply more physically difficult for men to express their emotions. Women, on the other hand, have centers of emotion on both sides of the brain. There are also more exchanges from side to side because they have more connecting fibers. This makes it easier for a woman to put her emotions into words and then express those words. This also explains why women find it more difficult to separate emotion from logic. Having emotional function residing on both sides of her brain causes a woman's practical reasoning to be connected to emotional responses. Furthermore, when women are processing emotional reactions, research has proven that they have 15 percent more blood flow to the brain, making the brain more active when processing feelings. Men, who have no emotional function on the left side, experience practical concrete situations without any emotional interference.

Men are frequently frustrated when women don't communicate directly. They complain that women don't come out and say what they mean. Women are just as frustrated when they ask a man a question and he replies with a simple yes or no, rather than an explanation. There is a physical reason for this as well. Centers of vocabulary reside in different places in male and female brains. Male brain functions for these abilities are in the left hemisphere (both front and back), making them more specific. A woman's vocabulary functions lie on both sides of her brain (both left and right as well as front and back), resulting in a lessened ability to clearly express herself. Women also talk more then men. Why? A larger percentage of the female brain is devoted to word production and word usage than a male brain. In fact, the typical man uses half the words a woman does.

Recent studies have used MRIs (magnetic resonance imaging), PETs (positronic emission tomography), and SPECTs (single photon emission computed tomography) to scan and take "pictures" of the brain at work. These pictures show some significant differences in how men and women use their brains. This could also explain their different approaches to communication. Women tend to use many parts of their brain at the same time to perform a task, while men use only one part of their brain. Additional studies show that when men are resting, their brain activity is very low. A woman's resting brain is still very active. This may explain why a man finds it easier to focus on a specific task, while a woman often appears to be doing several things at once. In general, it has been found that men tend to use (and therefore develop) the left side of their brain more than the right side, while the opposite is true of women. Since the left hemisphere tends to "see" specifics, men focus on just one specific aspect of a situation, often the one that affects them personally, at a time. The right hemisphere tends to "see" the big picture, which means women are more prone to look at a situation overall and from several different viewpoints. This also explains why it appears to take women so long to make a decision. They literally need more time to "make up their mind" since their brains are looking at the situation from many more angles.

Just from this short discussion of "brain differences" you can begin to see that many of the difficulties between the sexes are related to how our brains function. It would be extremely prejudicial and untrue to say one type of brain functions the "right" way, implying that the other type of brain functions the "wrong" way. It is quite simply the way nature has programmed us physically. Another significant physical influence on gender is hormones. In fact, it is the effect hormones have on the brain that is responsible for programming our different brain functions in the first place.

Hormones

There are three types of hormones that have been identified. They are *androgens*, *estrogen*, and *progesterone*. Androgens, which include testosterone, are male hormones, and estrogen and progesterone are female hormones. In normal individuals, all three types of hormones exist regardless of sex. Women typically have between one-tenth and one-third the amount of testosterone of the average man. A man's system also produces small amounts of female hormones. During gestation, a fetus receives varying amounts of these hormones that "wash" its body and brain. Typically, during the third and sixth month of pregnancy there is a surge of hormones released that bombards the developing fetus's brain. The purpose of these additional hormones is to organize the body and brain so it will function as male or female.

Suppose the developing fetus is genetically female. If she receives the right amount of female hormones, she will possess a body and brain that thinks, acts, and looks feminine. A developing male child who receives the proper amount of androgens develops in a masculine way. What if for some reason (for example: a mother going through menopause) the developing fetus takes in more of the opposite sex hormone? In a male, this may cause him to *think* more like a she, and vice versa for a female. This could affect behavior and communication as well.

Another important function of hormones is to coordinate the body and brain functions it has organized. This takes place during puberty, when an increase in hormones activates the reproductive system in both boys and girls. As you have no doubt noticed, this is a period of life when gender differences become even more pronounced. Later in life, as we age, hormone production slows down and the opposite begins to occur. While men remain men and women remain women as they age, men and women begin to think and react in more similar ways. Now let's take a look at what effect hormones have on our communication.

Male hormones cause increases in behaviors such as aggression, competition, self-assertion, self-confidence, and self-reliance. Female hormones decrease the very same behaviors. Look closely and you will easily see how hormones that affect our behaviors can also affect communication. Men tend to be more aggressive than women, a physiological fact. In communication this leads to men using language that is stronger, more direct, and frequently commanding. Women react to this communication as if men are purposely ordering them about. Men are more self-reliant, which means they are less likely to ask for assistance or to talk about problems, behaviors that women frequently interpret as "shutting them out" or being stubborn. Women, due to hormonal influences, are less confident and more nurturing and often want men to reassure them. Think about Susan and Jason and their many misunderstandings. These can be accounted for by hormones. Both Susan and Jason are confused and become angry at times. They don't understand each other's behavior. They have tried to communicate with each other. Neither one of them intended to start a fight. The fact is both of them were communicating according to typical gender style, and neither of them understood what was going on. If you think about it for a moment, you can probably think of several scenarios you have been involved in that can be traced to physiology and hormones. Let's examine another effect that hormones have on gender communication.

Both men and women are aware that hormones are responsible for what has been labeled PMS, premenstrual syndrome. Women who suffer from this ailment are moody and temperamental days prior to the onset of their monthly cycle. Their communication and behavior is affected by changing hormonal levels in the blood system. This is not something women have control over, and they can only treat the symptoms, not the cause. Similar reactions occur when a woman reaches menopause, a time when hormones decrease. It is less commonly known that men also go through a cycle of adjusting hormonal levels, which also affects their behavior. These cycles fluctuate more than female cycles, and are being documented in numerous studies. In fact there is even evidence that points to what is being labeled "male menopause." When testosterone levels are at their peak in a man's cycle, he tends to be more aggressive, more self-absorbed, and demonstrate other behaviors stimulated by testosterone, all of which affect his communication and ultimately his relationships. As a man ages, these hormones decrease as do the corresponding behaviors. As is true for women, these behavioral patterns are caused by hormones over which a man has no control. He too can only treat the symptoms.

Brain Chemicals

Finally, there is one additional physical influence we need to examine, chemicals in the brain. **Serotonin** is a chemical that, when released into the blood stream, produces a calming effect. Male serotonin levels are almost always lower than female levels. This results in males being more impulsive than females, as they are less calm most of the time. **Oxytocin,** known as the "bonding chemical," is the second chemical in the brain that influences gender behaviors. The higher the level of oxytocin in a person's blood stream, the less aggressive he or she is. Those with high levels of this chemical are also more empathetic and tend to seek out others, forming close relationships. Care to guess which gender typically has a higher level of oxytocin? Yes, women do. Men's lower levels of both serotonin and oxytocin may explain why men tend to "act first and talk later."

We hope the examples and explanations above help you to understand that many behaviors exhibited by men and women are not done so intentionally. In an attempt to help you understand, we have greatly simplified some very complex biological functions. We also want you to realize that we aren't suggesting that you have to act a certain way because of your brain geography, or because of the levels and types of hormone and chemicals in your blood stream. Our purpose is to make you more aware of why we may act the way we do with respect to gender. This knowledge may better equip you to empathize with a member of the opposite gender. Empathy is a useful communication tool. We've only scratched the surface of physiological differences that science has discovered. In the future, it is likely there will be many more discoveries that will impact our understanding of gender communication. These physical influences aren't the only influences on gender. There are environmental influences as well.

Activity for Further Understanding

What Gender Is Your Brain?

You can get an idea whether you tend to think in a predominately male or female style by answering and scoring this quiz. While you may be physically a member of one sex, your "brain layout" may result in you thinking more in the manner of the opposite sex. (Remember our earlier reference to hormones "washing" the developing fetus.)

Read the following personality traits and rate each using the following scale:

1 = you behave this way 0% of the time (very rarely)
3 = you behave this way 50% of the time (half the time)
5 = you behave this way 100% of the time (most of the time)

1. Talk about your emotions
2. Make decisions quickly
3. Put other peoples needs and wants before your own
4. Take risks physically and emotionally
5. Recognize voices of people you have only talked to a few times
6. Can point to the east with little thought
7. Try to help others even when not asked
8. Are competitive in most situations
9. Prefer intimate gatherings to large parties
10. Can easily back a car into a tight parking space
11. Can quickly locate where a sound is coming from
12. Find it easy to "tune out" external noise
13. Are sympathetic
14. Are ambitious
15. Show affection for others
16. Prefer to be the leader
17. Remember names and faces of people you have just met
18. Are independent
19. Spend time on your appearance
20. Are aggressive in actions and words

To determine your score, add up all your answers to the even numbered questions (2-4-6-8, etc.). Then tally the odd numbered questions (1-3-5-7, etc.). The even total is your masculine score and the odd total is your feminine score. If your even score is significantly higher than your odd score (+10 or more) then you probably behave according to male brain patterns. If your odd score is significantly higher than your even score (+10 or more) then you probably behave according to female brain patterns. The greater the difference between your even and odd scores, the more likely you are to find communication with the opposite gender confusing and even frustrating. You probably cross communicate frequently. The closer the tallies are, the more balanced you are, meaning you probably don't cross communicate as often as others might.

Please note that this quiz, while based on reputable research, is incapable of measuring deeper differences that would more accurately identify brain gender. It does provide some information that may be helpful as you attempt to improve your gender communication. In addition it should be noted that brain "gender" has nothing to do with sexual preference. Homosexuals typically score no differently in regards to brain gender than heterosexuals.

The Nurture Argument

More commonly known by many people are environmental influences from societal or cultural factors. This is the *nurture* argument. If you stop and think about it, you can list numerous influences on how you think, act, and communicate based on what you have been taught about gender roles. In chapter 5 we discussed several factors that influence the development of your self-concept such as reflected appraisal and social comparisons. These same forces have helped shape your gender identification and how you communicate in the context of that gender. While infants may be born with certain *physiological* determiners that affect how they act, the way people communicate with us from birth teaches us what is acceptable behavior for our gender.

While cultures vary in their perception of gender roles, we will confine our discussion to North American culture. It is important to remember that just because our culture perceives certain behaviors to be masculine or feminine, other cultures may not. For example, while North Americans generally view crying in public as acceptable for women but not for men, there are cultures where men are not seen as feminine when they cry. In North America we tend to believe that women are more nurturing and assign them caregiving roles. There are, however, other cultures that assign that role to men or even young boys.

We learn gender behaviors from others, both verbally and nonverbally. There is a vast amount of research that shows adults treat baby boys differently than baby girls even moments after their birth. Little boys are handled more roughly by both men and women. Little girls are talked to more than little boys. Up to the age of four or five, mothers and fathers typically hug and kiss children of both sexes. Around school age this changes, particularly when it comes to fathers and sons. Dad begins to teach his son masculine behavior, which probably includes saying "men don't hug and kiss men." Boys who exhibit what our society labels feminine traits are often teased and labeled a sissy. Girls who act in more masculine ways are labeled tomboys. When Mom praises her daughter for keeping her new outfit clean or tells her son thank you for being such a strong little man when he carries in the groceries, she is influencing her children to respond in (stereotypical) gender style. Teachers and other adults who interact with children continue to reinforce these gender stereotypes, often punishing behaviors that are not gender appropriate. Although some of this is changing in our society, it is changing slowly. Even those who believe in equality of the sexes, and who attempt to treat children equally, admit that they find themselves reacting to nontypical gender behavior in a negative way.

Many new parents try not to reinforce their child's gender by buying them "gender neutral" toys. However, in our society little boys primarily play with cars and trucks, while little girls still feed and dress their dolls. Little girls tend to play with one or two other girls in noncompetitive play like "house," hopscotch, and jump rope, while young boys are more likely to participate in large groups or teams that play competitive games like baseball, super heroes, and "war." Even "gender neutral" parents tend to be uncomfortable with the thought of their son in an apron playing "tea party" or their daughters bringing home a snake. While the majority of women say they would not be disturbed if their sons played with dolls, men are more divided on the subject. Half of the men polled on this topic clearly indicated, "no son of mine will play with dolls." The other half weren't so certain. They indicated that while they may not care if their sons had dolls as toys, they wouldn't want them to play with them in public!

The media also influence gender identity. Magazines marketed to women focus on clothes, makeup, cooking, and weight loss. Men's magazines concentrate on sports, vehicles, sex, and physically attractive women. TV shows and movies reinforce gender roles by carrying the message that real men act a certain way and real women act the opposite. A commercial that showed men saying, "do I look fat in this" and "I know my hips are too big but I can't help it . . . I get them from my mother," was received by the viewing public as amusing. Everyone knows that generally men would never say those things; instead those are statements women make. Another ad showed a woman sitting on a bed, dressed just in a man's shirt. She stands up, looks in a full-length mirror, and puts a man's hat on her head, just as the phone rings. She answers it and says, "Honey I was just thinking about you." Now suppose we change the gender of the person in this commercial. A man sits on the bed dressed only in a woman's blouse. He looks in the mirror, places a frilly feminine hat on his head, and answers the phone with the same line. The second scenario, unlike the real commercial, probably seems funny or inappropriate to you. Why? The answer is gender training. We've learned that some behaviors are appropriate or acceptable, but others are not, even if they are approached in an amusing manner.

These examples, and countless others that you can add on your own, show that we are influenced by what society considers male or female

Activity for Further Understanding

Gender Journal

For one week, keep a journal of the positive and negative reinforcement you receive from others pertaining to any gender behavior. Record these observations and who was involved. You should also make note of how you reacted to messages from others. At the end of the week summarize what you have found. Examine your behaviors and how the reaction to those behaviors has influenced your self-concept and self-esteem.

behavior. We are rewarded for acting like we "should" and frequently punished in some way when we act like we shouldn't. This obviously affects our communication.

We have offered these very general looks at physiological and environmental influences to give you some insight as to why men and women think, act, and communicate differently. Now that we understand why men and women are different, we need to understand how these differences affect communication so we can improve our gender communication.

Problems with Gender Communication

As mentioned previously, we have identified several differences between men and women that result in opposite thoughts and behaviors. When we are using our own gender style to communicate with the opposite gender, we frequently **cross-communicate**. The message received will be interpreted in the opposite way in which the sender intended. Furthermore, the receiver has the tendency to believe the message they get is what the sender intended. This isn't necessarily true; this results in misunderstandings.

Consider the situation Susan and Jason found themselves in at the beginning of this chapter. Susan wanted Jason to know she loved him. If *she* had a problem she'd want to talk about it and would want Jason to listen, showing he cared. She assumed that since he obviously was grappling with a problem, he'd want her to help. To show someone you care and want to help, you ask a lot of questions, encourage the other person to talk, and listen. So that's what she did, as most women would. Jason, however, wanted her to trust him to work out what was bothering him alone. To Jason, when you trust someone, you don't interrogate him with a lot of questions. You leave him alone, knowing he will choose the best solution. Most men would agree with Jason. Susan's questions were interpreted by Jason as distrust in his ability to solve the problem. The result was cross-communication. He believed she had attacked his self-esteem, which wasn't her intent but was the message he received.

The frequency with which men and women cross-communicate is probably the most significant reason why there are misunderstandings between them. While we certainly have misunderstandings with our same-gender friends, those between the genders are much more common and typically result in more arguments and complications. Being aware of gender differences will help us approach gender communication more effectively and decrease cross-communication.

Look at the following lists. Each contains gender characteristics for each gender. Read each list to get an idea of gender-specific characteristics and then compare them across to see what differences might cause gender cross-communication.

Women	*Men*
1. Are other-centered	1. Are self-centered
2. Fear abandonment	2. Fear engulfment
3. Identify with people	3. Identify with work
4. Need to know others care	4. Need to know they are trusted
5. Need others' validation of self and ideas	5. Need simple approval of self and ideas
6. Relate emotionally to most situations	6. Relate logically to most situations
7. Need frequent reassurance about themselves and their actions	7. Need encouragement to start but then want to be left alone
8. Attempt to avoid conflict	8. Often seek competition
9. Want to know they are understood	9. Want to know they are accepted
10. Are love-oriented (emotional)	10. Are sex-oriented (physical)

One of the biggest problems in cross-communication is what each gender believes is the purpose of communication. Men predominately consider (and use) communication to share information. Women mainly use communication to evaluate relationship climates. This typically results in cross-communication. Let's illustrate this concept by projecting Susan and Jason into the future.

Jason and Susan are about to celebrate their twentieth wedding anniversary. Susan wants them to reaffirm their vows by having another wedding and inviting friends and family to be witnesses. When she mentions it to Jason and asks for his opinion, he replies he doesn't want to do that. Susan wants to know why, and Jason says, "It'll be a waste of money." Jason is being honest and direct. In his opinion, Susan made a suggestion and wanted to know what he thought. He has now answered her and considers the subject closed. He is confused and annoyed when Susan begins to cry like he has attacked her. He says, "What's wrong?" Susan replies that if he doesn't know she isn't going to tell him. Jason shrugs, mutters "women," and goes to the garage to work on his car. Susan, looking like she has barely survived a nuclear disaster, appears at the garage door. She looks at Jason and says, "You don't love me anymore." Jason, who is focused on finding out why the car has been making a clicking noise, looks up, smiles, and says, "Oh hey, get me a beer." Susan leaves, and when she doesn't come back, Jason continues to work on the car. Later he goes into the bedroom where Susan is obviously still hurting and angry. She asks, "Why don't you love me anymore, what have I done?" Jason is totally confused. Why does she think he doesn't love her any more? After all, he's been married to her for twenty years, pays the bills, and is pretty sure he told her he loved her just last week.

What happened here? Jason thought Susan was asking a direct question, "Do you want to reaffirm our wedding vows for our anniversary?" He answered, "No," which is what Jason considered an honest and factual response. Susan, on the other hand was "relationship checking." She wanted to be reassured that even after twenty years of marriage, he still loved her and would marry her all over again. Not only did his curt response indicate to Susan that things may not be okay between them, but his lack of empathy also resulted in her feeling unloved. While the men reading this may think this illustration is contrived and unrealistic, we think the women reading this will understand completely, which is another example of cross-communication! The opposite is also true as to Jason's confusion over Susan's inability to accept "No" as a legitimate acceptable answer. After all, she asked a question, he answered (he was listening and hadn't ignored her). He had communicated in a perfectly acceptable manner. His intention hadn't been to upset her. We bet the men can relate to this and have often muttered "women"!

Perhaps the difference that causes the most cross-communication is how we view the world. Since men tend to focus on one specific thing at a time versus a woman's ability to multitask, men and women often misunderstand each other. Men are more self-focused (not to be confused with selfish) while women are other-focused.

In the male world it is very important to solve problems as an individual. This is how a man gains self-esteem, working things out on his own. The result is a man, being more self-focused and self-reliant, will approach the problem as a puzzle to solve. He looks at how different outcomes will affect *him*. In order to do this, he needs private space and time to work out his solution. He may go shoot some hoops, go to the garage to work on a project, or go for a run. Men trust themselves to come up with a good solution on their own and fix what is broken. Women, on the other hand, approach problem situations very differently.

Women are other-focused, which means they look at the effect something will have on many, including themselves. They boost their self-esteem from how well their relationships are working. Where men need to know they are trusted, women need to know they are cared about. In order to resolve a conflict or find a solution, a woman needs to talk about it with others who care. She is not asking for someone to fix it for her; she just wants the other person to listen so she can sort out all the information she has gathered. With these opposite ways of looking at things, you can see why cross-communication occurs and can be so confusing and frustrating for both genders.

Suggestions for Avoiding Cross-Communication

We've shared some of the biggest problems that occur daily between men and women when they communicate. Now that you are aware of some of the differences between the genders, you should be able to see more clearly what was happening the last time you experienced cross-communication. The following suggestions may help you next time you are communicating with a member of the opposite sex.

The Opaque Rule

It is probably safe to assume that most of you can quote the Golden Rule. "Do unto others as you would have them do unto you." While this is good advice in many cases, as in treating people respectfully because that's how you wish to be treated, it often is the cause of gender misunderstandings between men and women. In the story at the beginning of the chapter, Susan was treating Jason as she would have expected Jason to treat her in the same situation, following the Golden Rule! The problem is that *wasn't* what Jason wanted. The same would have been true if the situation had been reversed.

We suggest a new rule called the **opaque rule**. Opaque means that which cannot be seen through. By not assuming others want to be treated the way we want to be treated if we were both faced with the same situation, we will more likely avoid misunderstanding or conflict when confronting the opposite gender. It is, "Do unto others as they would have done unto themselves." In other words, women already communicate with other women in a way both can understand. The same is true for men with other men. There are fewer intragender communication breakdowns. Just think about how many times men say, "I just can't understand women" or "Women, can't live with them, can't live without them." Consider the frequency that women say "Men!" or "You [the *you* being male] just don't understand!" Therefore, it is logical that if women were to communicate like men and vice versa, there will be less cross-communication between them. Read the following scenario to help understand why the Golden Rule doesn't always work.

When I (Tracey) am sick with a cold, I like to have someone around who will pamper me and give me chicken soup. When Mary (my coauthor and friend) is sick, she doesn't want anyone around and hates chicken soup. So when Mary becomes ill, I go to her house with tissues, sympathy, and homemade chicken soup. My intent is to follow the Golden Rule and treat her the way I like to be treated. Now what's wrong with that? As we'll discuss in the next chapter, we don't always interpret things the same way. Given Mary's desire to be left alone when ill and her dislike of chicken soup (no matter how lovingly made), it is likely she isn't going to be too pleased with my visit. Mary will probably be civil but not as friendly as usual and her nonverbals will definitely say, "go away." My present of chicken soup will be received less enthusiastically than I thought it would be. I'll probably leave wondering why she was angry with me, while Mary goes back to bed wondering why I was such a nuisance.

The outcome of such an encounter is hardly what I had in mind when I went to Mary's house. She may also be annoyed that someone who knows her so well would make such efforts to pamper her. There has been a misunderstanding simply because I was following the Golden Rule, do unto others as you would have them do unto you. This is exactly what happens so frequently in gender communication. Men treat women as they (men) want to be treated, believing they are doing what is right, and women respond as if they have been seriously injured. When women treat men like they (women) want to be treated, men often interpret it as an attack on their self-esteem or ability to achieve a goal. On the other hand, using the *opaque rule*, not assuming we can "see" another's desires as our own, we use empathy to facilitate effective communication. Let's go back to the chicken soup example. I'm on my way out the door with tissues, sympathy, and soup for Mary. I stop, and by applying the opaque rule, real- ize that Mary doesn't want these things. She doesn't want anything but to be left alone! Oh well, at least I have dinner ready for tonight! This same application works with men and women. If Susan and Jason had been more aware of gender traits at work here, they might have avoided this sit- uation by employing the opaque rule: Don't assume you can "see" others' desires and that those desires are the same as yours. Susan would have "seen" that just because she would want help, Jason didn't!

Applying the Opaque Rule

A word of caution, or maybe a reminder, is important at this time. All communication between men and women isn't necessarily cross-com- munication due to gender differences. There are of course many instances when we are capable of communicating very effectively with each other. There are other times that misunderstandings occur between men and women that aren't related to gender. However, since gender differences are frequently a cause of confusion and misinterpretation between the sexes, applying the opaque rule should result in more effective communication in many cases. Following the steps listed below will help you treat others as *they* want to be treated, increase empathy, and lessen misunderstandings:

- *Step One: Be aware.* Being aware of the gender traits that may be affecting the conversation means you have to monitor what is occurring. If the reaction you are getting seems to be very different from your intent, bells should go off. Cross-communication may be at work. Monitoring requires some effort because your normal responses are typical of the way you communicate and seem natural to you. Normally you wouldn't be aware that you are being perceived differently. The first step to improvement and satisfaction is awareness.

- *Step Two: Be empathic.* Throughout this text we have stressed how important empathy is to effective communication. If you can understand what the other person's verbal and nonverbal messages really mean and have some idea why the person has certain reactions, you will be better equipped to communicate with that person. This is especially important in gender communication situations. Since men and women relate to and communicate very differently, it is essential to have some background and understanding of why they may be acting the way they are. Look at it from their point of view. Admittedly, because women already tend to be other-focused, this may be easier for them than it is for men, who tend to be self-focused. However, men can approach empathy more easily if they realize that what is affecting their opposite-gender partner eventually will affect them too.

- *Step Three: Clearly explain your understanding.* Paraphrase what you believe he or she is saying. Once the person realizes that you understand, use I language to express your agreement or disagreement. She could say to him, "Honey, I can see you're trying to sort some things out, so I won't bother you. I would appreciate it if after you've thought about it, you would talk to me. I want you to know I care about you, and I trust you to come up with what seems best. I may not agree with it, but if we talk later, we'll see if we can agree and can go from there." Notice she shows she understands his need for time and trusts him to come back to her later to discuss it. She also lets him know she cares, which satisfies her need to be other-focused without interfering with his need to be self-focused.

Applying the opaque rule effectively encourages communication and avoids cross-communication. You absolutely have to deal with others' perceptions because that is the reality *they* are living. Remembering that their perceptions and realities may be different from yours, as in the case of gender, will help you be a more effective communicator.

Tips for Effective Gender Communication

Before we leave this unit, we'd like to offer some quick tips for effective gender communication. We have barely scratched the surface of this important communication key. If you choose to pursue improvement of your communication with the opposite gender, we briefly offer some very practical suggestions. We call them quick tips.

Quick Tips for Men

1. ***Reassure her often that you care about her.*** Women really do need to hear "I love you" often. Show you care by doing things that *she* believes show you care. They may not be the same things *you* think show caring.

2. ***Don't "fix" her problems.*** Remember, a woman fixes her own problems by sorting them out through talking. When she asks for your help, she is really *only* asking you to listen. A man who talks about his problems is perceived by other men to be asking for help. They also assume he must really need it or he wouldn't be asking. Admitting you need help, in the masculine world, is admitting defeat. It says, "I can't solve this on my own." He's just lost a rung on the male hierarchical ladder. He didn't compete as well. Women don't think this way. If you just show you care by listening, she'll work it out. The added benefit is you will be her hero, and she'll show she appreciates your help, even though you didn't offer a solution.

3. ***Listen the way she thinks you should.*** Men usually get a bad rap for being inattentive listeners. While there is research to show that men do tend to listen less often then women, there is another factor at work. Even when men are listening, they don't look like women think someone who is listening should look. If you don't look like you are listening, then women assume you aren't! In other words men need to show they are listening in a way a woman will understand. Women look at each other when they listen. They respond with nonverbals like facial expressions and nods. They say things like "uh-huh" and "mmmm." They rarely interrupt the speaker. One of the most effective things you can do in gender communication is learn to listen to a woman the way she listens to others.

4. *Remember that men and women keep score differently.* Men think that because they provide an income that pays the bills (or part of them) they are receiving hundreds of points every week. When you fix her car or suggest she take it to the mechanic you are implying you love her, and that's worth points. Men frequently are very frustrated when women accuse them of not being supportive or caring when they truly believe their actions have earned them a lot of points in the gender bank. It doesn't work that way. You work, and that's one point (female perception). You spent Saturday with the kids so she could go shopping with her mom, that's one point. In other words, you think you're a millionaire and one little flaw or situation shouldn't hurt your account with her very much. She, on the other hand, is preparing to tell you that you're overdrawn, and you even owe her several insufficient funds' fees.

5. *Remember that shopping is a social occasion.* Most of the time shopping (other than for groceries) for women is a fun time. It involves dressing a certain way, talking, having lunch, maybe taking in a movie later, and only partly involves buying things. It is a process, not an outcome. It is just the opposite for most men. Men go shopping for a very specific outcome, to purchase something they need. We call this the "get in and get out" approach to shopping. It goes like this: Find the nearest parking place to the exact door you need. Once in the store, go directly to the aisles that contain the items you desire. Grab the items, check out, and go home. There is no contemplating what to wear, who should come with you, and where to eat, or asking your companion if the item you've picked out is the right choice. Remember that her way may not be the way you shop, but that doesn't make it wrong. Going shopping with her might show you care, but rushing her through the process will send the opposite message and deduct more points from the gender bank.

Quick Tips for Women

1. *Be more direct.* Stop all the hinting and deep sighs. Say what you mean even if that means figuring it out before, instead of while, you talk to him. Men are more focused and frequently aren't aware of all those nonverbal signs you are giving. You think that if he cared he'd notice them and do something about it (the way you want it done of course), but he doesn't. Say, "Will you fix the garbage disposal?" not "Can you fix it?" Women often ask men if they can do something. When he answers yes, she thinks he's agreed to fix it. No, he is saying he has the ability or skill to fix it. Of course he *can* fix it. He didn't say he would. Women then get angry when the disposal still isn't working, and he's confused because he

doesn't remember saying he'd fix it. However, asking him if he *will* fix it is a request for a specific answer. "Yes," "no," or "yes, but not now" will be the answer. We realize this may sound like a picky point, as we (your authors) did when we were first introduced to this idea. However, we not only have found it works, but men have told us it makes it much easier to understand when we are asking for help. Also, clearly mark anniversaries, birthdays, and social engagements on the calendar in such a way that he will know exactly what is occurring. A poster size calendar, marked in permanent marker hung on his garage wall will help him to remember.

2. ***Don't follow him.*** This may be one of the behaviors that bug men the most about women. He needs self-time to solve a problem or work something out, and here is this woman (who supposedly likes and cares about him) preventing him from doing what he has to do. She obviously is asking for a reaction; after all, any guy knows when to leave another guy alone. Remember most of the time he's going to get away from everybody, not just you. Don't assume the problem is about you. He does have other interests in his life. He hasn't abandoned you. He'll be back. Men, if you are reading this section you might help her out by acting like Arnold Schwarzenegger and saying "I'll be back." It seems obvious to you, but at the moment she's not too sure. If you follow a man he may react angrily even though you just wanted to help. The more you leave him alone, the quicker he will be back.

3. ***He said what he meant.*** Since men are able to focus more easily than women and are more direct communicators, they believe that what they said is a sufficient and truthful answer to what you asked. Men don't tend to elaborate when they say yes or no, and they don't understand why you keep asking them what they meant or how they feel about it. Men usually see communication as a means of sharing information. They view communication effectiveness as delivering clear content in a message. Women are usually more concerned about the relational message delivered. They are more likely to look for the bond or emotion implied in the message, which indicates the health of the relationship between the two people communicating. Ladies, when a man says yes or no, that's all it means!

4. ***Looking doesn't mean he wants to replace you.*** A student once said the thing he just couldn't understand about his girlfriend was why she got angry when he looked at other attractive women. He wasn't intending to touch, just to look. When asked, his girlfriend even admitted that the woman who had caught his attention was pretty, and he was simply appreciating the view. Then why was she angry? Didn't she understand that he appreci-

ated pretty women, and the fact that he was with her, chose to be with her, meant he found her the prettiest? In an indirect way, his admiration of other pretty women demonstrated how much he cared about her. We know you might be tempted not to believe this. No woman in her right mind (or right brain) would interpret this behavior as a compliment. But remember, women think very differently than men!

5. ***Never offer a man unsolicited advice.*** It may mean to you that you are showing how much you care, but it usually means just the opposite to him. Men only want suggestions when they ask for them and they'll be direct when they ask. You will know when he is asking: he'll say, "I need help," or "I need advice" (he won't hint). Don't read anything extra into a message. As we've said before, asking for help is admitting defeat in the male world. When you offer him help he hasn't asked for, he interprets it as losing face. He thinks you don't trust him to fix whatever it is. He may become defensive, and that rarely leads to effective communication. Women don't intend to send these messages to the men in their lives, but they frequently do.

Conclusion

No brief coverage of the many influences on our communication, from a gender perspective, could begin to do justice to this important subject. We don't mean to imply that because this (or any other chapter in the text) comes to an end, we have provided you with everything you may need to know. This is particularly true of gender communication. There is a lot more information available than we can present in such a quick overview. However, we believe we've helped you to begin that voyage. We've given you some things to think about and some suggestions for achieving your goals in achieving effective gender communication—another key to survival.

DISCUSSION QUESTIONS

1. In your opinion, which is more influential in gender: nature or nurture? Support your answer.

2. Explain a misunderstanding you had with a member of the opposite sex. List the gender-specific traits that you think were responsible.

3. Do you think using the opaque rule will make you a more effective communicator? Explain and support your answer.

4. Using the three reasons messages go astray (chapter 1), give an example for each caused by gender differences.

5. Choose a few gender characteristics from the comparison list in this chapter and explain how these can cause cross-communication.

KEY TERMS

corpus callosum   opaque rule
cross-communication   oxytocin
gender communication   serotonin

chapter eight

Perception

Double take . . . better look again!

CHAPTER HIGHLIGHTS

- Perception is the process of becoming aware of events, people, or situations through the use of the senses.
- We primarily use our senses to perceive elements in our surroundings and assign meaning to them.
- There are secondary physiological influences in the perception process as well.
- Our social situations and our lifestyle choices affect the perception process.
- Our perceptions are not always accurate.
- Mistakes in perception lead to stereotyping and misunderstandings.
- There are many challenges to the perception process.
- Controlling these challenges can decrease perceptual misunderstandings.
- Respecting perceptual differences is a key to survival.

Jason had been gone for over two hours. It was nearly 8:00 PM and Susan had been worried ever since he walked out. She hadn't thought that Jason's anger was directed at her. She thought he must have a problem at work. She knew that when work was on his mind Jason often seemed distracted. That's why she had offered to talk about it with him. Even when he said he was going out for a little while, she hadn't thought he was mad at her. Now she was sure he was angry with her! He said he'd be gone a "little while." Two hours wasn't a little while in Susan's mind, it was a long while.

Jason glanced at his watch. "Great," he thought, "it's not quite 8:00 PM yet." That meant he'd be able to shower and get home before 8:30. Having the gym so close was just one of the many things Jason loved about the condo. Another was the coffee shop on the corner of the block; he and Susan loved the mochas there. He'd have time to grab a couple and still get home to watch that video with Susan. Jason mentally congratulated himself on having come up with a solution during his workout. He'd decided what tactic he would take at the meeting on Monday. He had also burned off enough calories to treat himself to a mocha! He couldn't remember if Susan was on a diet this week or not so he'd take her one too. Jason didn't think she needed to lose weight anyway. He whistled as he walked home with their drinks. He was a lucky man. It was the weekend and he and Susan had promised each other they would spend it together. They'd agreed that neither one of them would bring any work home. He was happy his work problem was solved and looked forward to their evening of videos, mocha, and popcorn. Most of all he was happy to spend some uninterrupted time with Susan.

It was 8:30 and Susan was quite sure that Jason was angry with her and avoiding being alone with her. She didn't know why and that added fuel to her fire. "How dare he be angry with me! I haven't done anything for him to be angry about! I promised not to bring any work home and I didn't. He promised me that we'd just relax and watch videos tonight. He's the one who broke his promise." Susan looked at the clock. It was past 8:30. The whole evening was gone.

As Jason opened the door (no easy feat considering he was balancing two mochas) he was sure it was going to be a great night. He'd kept his word to only be gone a little while, and he was bringing Susan a surprise. Susan loved surprises, particularly chocolate ones! Smiling, he says, "I bring chocolate." Jason walks into the living room expecting to be greeted by a smiling Susan.

"You said you'd only be gone a little while! Now the whole night is shot. And why are you angry with me? You're the one who broke your promise! Is that mocha? Did you think bringing me a present would make up for running off and ruining the entire evening? I'm on a diet and you bring me mocha?! I thought you couldn't be any more inconsiderate than when you walked out. It appears I was wrong."

For a moment, Jason reconsiders marrying this woman standing in front of him. It sure isn't the Susan he was planning to marry!

What Is Perception?

Obviously, Susan and Jason's perceptions of the evening and time are vastly different. **Perception** is the process of becoming aware of events, objects, sounds, and smells and then labeling them. Our perceptions consist of our interpretations of what we see, feel, taste, touch, and smell and are based on past experiences and our personal environment. They are not necessarily fact, but they are how we view the world.

Some people say perception is a "first impression" of a situation. This is a little misleading, because some events and situations can be experienced a second and third time with new or changing elements. Do we continue to have first impressions, or do we add new information to an original impression and constantly reform it? Any time we become aware of new information we are experiencing the process of perception.

Our perceptions serve a number of functions. Everyday we gather information both consciously and unconsciously. We organize the data we gather so we can relate to everything and everyone around us. We then apply the information to what we already know; we assign meaning to our perceptions. However, our perceptions aren't necessarily factual. Jason's perception that he was coming home to a happy situation certainly wasn't a fact. Susan's perception that Jason was really angry with her wasn't a fact either. They had both experienced the same situation, but they had very different interpretations. This is because our perceptions are influenced by both physiological and psychological factors that are unique to each of us as individuals.

Primary Physiological Perceptual Influences

Our senses are the primary physiological influence in perception. We use our senses to help us become aware of new information or situations. Our senses are a part of our physical makeup; therefore they represent **physiological factors** that influence the perception process. These factors are visual, auditory, tactile, gustatory, and olfactory. Let's explore these sensory elements individually.

Visual: The Sense of Sight

Some people can make sense of information more easily if they can see something. These people perceive information primarily through sight. Observation of a new element or situation causes them to make decisions or judgments. For example, if this person walked into a doctor's office for the first time, he would see the lush green plants, the tasteful prints on the wall in gilded frames, the pastel wallpaper, the comfortable chairs, and the display of antique doctor's instruments on the table. This person would decide the waiting room was very comfortable based on all of the elements that he has seen. He relies on his vision to perceive the elements surrounding him.

Even the actual strength of our vision becomes a perceptual influence. For example when Tracey and her friend take a road trip, Tracey does all of the night driving. Her friend is supposed to be responsible for reading the map and giving directions. After six hours of driving, Tracey gets tired and crabby. She asks her friend how far to the next exit. Her friend, looking at the map, is not able to tell her until they have already driven past the exit. Tracey is angry, and her friend is embarrassed. A fight erupts. Finally, Tracey's friend yells, "I can't see the map! I need new glasses."

Auditory: The Sense of Hearing

Some people are able to perceive information more effectively by using their ears. They will use their sense of hearing to obtain information and make a decision about a new situation. Let's take a person with auditory perception to the same doctor's office. This time, however, upon entering the waiting room, our patient notices soft music playing over an intercom. She hears the rhythmic clicking of the receptionist's fingers on the computer keyboard and the soothing sounds of the fish aquarium filter in the corner. There is a water cooler in the other corner, and its occasional bubbling is very melodic to her. She senses the room as being very comfortable and inviting based on what she hears. This is a different perception than our visual friend's perception even though their analysis is the same.

Even our physical hearing is a factor. If we are hearing impaired, have water in our ears from swimming, or can't clearly hear what is being said, it can affect our perception. We try to "fill in" what we thought we heard. Also, our perception of sound levels is a factor here. Mary's children love to listen to their CDs at full volume. They add the Karaoke machine, their voices, their friend's voices, and by the time all is said and done, the pets begin to howl in "harmony" with the "music." If Mary tells them to "Turn that music down," they respond with, "Mommmm, we won't be able to hear it then." Talk about auditory perceptual difference!

Tactile: The Sense of Touch

There are others who perceive information primarily through touch. Whenever these people encounter a new situation, they rely on their sense of touch to obtain the information they need to perceive the new experience. Let's take the tactile person to the same doctor. When this patient walks into the room, he experiences a "sense" of calm when he touches the smooth, cool counter surface. He sits down when asked to do so, and sinks deeply into a plush leather chair. It feels cool and soft to his skin, and he is very comfortable. He is reassured by this sensation. Reassurance is what he expected from the doctor's office, as it gives him a sense that the doctor is competent. He is comfortable and feeling very well indeed. His decision was arrived at from yet a different set of stimuli than that of either our visual or auditory friends. Our actual fingertips can provide an influencing factor in perception. Think about people who buy cars with leather seats because they feel cool and slick. This is tactile perceptual influence.

Gustatory: The Sense of Taste

Although taste does not tend to be one of the primary ways people perceive information, it is an influence. Each person has a unique body chemistry that causes diverse reactions and opinions related to taste. Think about the flavor of something you didn't like as a child but developed a taste for as you got older. Was the taste of liver awful and bitter? Did you think the same about your first taste of coffee or tea? Think of an infant's face when she is trying a new food for the first time. Consider the taste of various alcoholic beverages. Most children do not like any of these tastes, but as they grow older their likes and dislikes relevant to the taste of an item change. Why is there a change? What is different? Will this cause a change in our perception? How can I like the taste of something when I'm 25 that I hated when I was five? Usually there has been a change in our body chemistry over time; we didn't necessarily learn to like an item, but our body chemistry has changed, causing a shift in our perception. Our gustatory, or taste-oriented, friend is very comfortable when she sits down in the waiting room, because she has popped a complimentary mint into her mouth. The soothing taste calms her nerves and makes her feel pleasant and relaxed.

Olfactory: The Sense of Smell

The last sense is that of smell. While the sense of smell is also not a primary perception mode, it does affect our perceptions. Think about odors for a moment. While we may agree on what smells good or bad in some instances (flowers versus garbage), chances are you have had disagreements with others about a particular odor. Studies show that our age and sex play an important role in our perception of various smells. Men and children tend to like the smell of sweet things more than women. Children like odors that adults find offensive. However, these differences in perception are linked directly to the chemical makeup of our bodies just as our differences in taste are. Let's take an olfactory (smell) friend to that very same doctor's office. Our olfactory patient is comfortable the moment he opens the office door, because he smells freshly brewed coffee instead of medicine. After all, any place that offers coffee that smells that good couldn't be all bad!

Secondary Physiological Perceptual Influences

There are additional physiological factors that can have an effect on the perception process. These factors are often found in the atmosphere surrounding us. They are elements that have a direct effect on our physical bodies and usually are secondary to our senses. Such factors might include temperature, height, weight, fatigue, hunger, or our overall physical health at the moment we are experiencing an event. Before we discuss these elements further, think about what things you would notice in your immediate surroundings. Which sensory mode do you use most often? How would this affect you when combined with the following elements?

Temperature

Hot and cold seem like straightforward factual conclusions. Nothing could be further from the truth. One hundred degrees Fahrenheit is factual; "that's hot" is a perceptual opinion. Our perception of temperature is based on a number of physical reactions: our metabolic rate, how much we perspire, the thickness of our skin, and so forth. These factors vary from person to person and determine how we interpret temperature. Here's an example. Mary's family installed a pool last summer. During a heat wave in the Midwest (there were hundred-degree days), the kids wanted to swim every day. They would get in the water and scream, "It's sooooo cold, brrrrr!" Mary, on the other hand, would get in the water and think it was cool and refreshing. What could be more perfect to ward off the heat than a refreshing dip in the pool? They were experiencing eighty-five degree water. However, since the water was almost twenty degrees cooler than the outside air, and fifteen degrees cooler than their body temperatures, Mary's daughters thought they were swimming in the Arctic Ocean! It didn't stop them from swimming, but their perception was vastly different from Mary's.

Height and Weight

We are acutely aware of our own size (height and weight). We also perceive other people based on how they measure up (or down). Mary once taught with a close friend and colleague at a university one summer; both were in the same room at all times. She, being five foot three, considers herself of average height. Her colleague, being six foot five, was tall, but not, in her perception, abnormally so for a man. While the students usually referred to them by their first names, they were surprised when they often heard the students talking to one another about the pixie and the giant. Together, their height skewed the class perception of normal height. Mary was perceived as very short and her colleague as exceptionally tall! Perhaps an even better example of perceptual difference relevant to height or weight comes from children. Literally seeing things through the eyes of a child changes how we view the world. Everything seems large to children. To a child, a person who has a slim build may not seem any different weight-wise than a person who is fifty pounds overweight. To the child, both people seem large. Try sitting on the floor for a moment before you read any further. Look around. Does your position affect the way you view the room? It should seem skewed and out of proportion to you, all a matter of perception.

Fatigue

When we are tired, we perceive things differently than when we are alert and full of energy. Think of that ten-page term paper you typed last week. The first eight pages were a breeze. You typed them in one afternoon with only two breaks for a diet cola. The last two pages were torture because you waited until midnight the night before the paper was due to type them. You just had to watch that science fiction movie first! You were tired, and those pages were awful. You used the same word processor, the same fingers, and the same room and lights for the last two pages as you did for the first eight. The difference is fatigue. If we lack energy due to lack of sleep or because of overexertion, we will tend to perceive simple tasks as strenuous. Under normal circumstances we would easily be able to accomplish these same tasks. This is also apparent when a "day" person and a "night" person attempt to communicate at six in the morning or twelve at night. Fatigue affects the physical body and is therefore a physiological factor that influences perception.

Hunger

When we are hungry and our body needs nourishment, we will perceive things differently than if we have just eaten and our bodies are satisfied. Food and water are two of our basic needs. Therefore, if we are hungry, our bodies will concentrate on this physical need before anything else. Mothers and fathers know that when an infant is hungry, the only way to quiet the child is to feed her. No amount of bouncing or soothing will do; she wants to eat, and she wants to eat now! Adults aren't much different, although we might be able to go longer without food. If we are hungry for a long period of time, we can't focus on anything except when we are going to eat our next meal. Because food is a basic, primary need for human beings, when this need is not met we will put our energies into satisfying our hunger before we worry about anything else. Did you ever notice that if dinner is late, tempers will flare, people will argue, and fights will begin? If you need to talk to another person, and that person is hungry, we suggest you feed him first. This is another physical factor that influences our perceptions. Let's eat first and talk later!

Overall Health

If you are physically ill with a headache, the flu, or a cold, you will perceive things much differently than when you are in the peak of health. Speaking from a purely physical standpoint, our health is a major factor in our perceptual process. Surely you have observed that people who aren't feeling their best seem crabby and short-tempered. They don't see (perceive) things the way they did yesterday or even an hour earlier, before the ailment hit. Since our health and well-being become of primary importance to us, we often find it difficult to concentrate on anything other than how miserable we are feeling. Even though we may be capable of functioning, as opposed to being sick enough to be in bed, our perceptual processes are severely affected. We think less clearly, have a shorter attention span, and tend to resent trying to accomplish anything other than getting well. It is best to refrain from important decisions, conversations, or the like until we are better and feeling up to par. This is because our perceptions before and during these events will be affected by our ill health.

We have finished examining the many physiological factors that can influence the perception process. These factors affect our physical bodies, but because we cannot separate our bodies from our minds, our perceptions will be affected by psychological influences as well. There are many other factors to discuss that fall under this category of psychological factors. These are generally factors that we associate with mindsets or mental choices and can be categorized into two groups: social situations and lifestyle choices.

Psychological Perceptual Influences

Psychological factors are those that result in our thinking a particular way about a situation or event. These factors are a part of our everyday lives because they have become fixed in our heads. They have become second nature to us so that we rarely give them much thought. We automatically react to situations with perceptions based on these social and lifestyle experiences. Let's first explore social situations to see how they influence our perceptions.

Social Situations

We are influenced on a regular basis by **social situations**, those experiences and encounters that incorporate people in society and their viewpoints. Religious preference, family heritage, cultural background, and economic status are all elements that are socially derived. Even gender can impose a bias and skew our perceptions, as we learned in the previous chapter. To better understand how social influences affect our perceptions, let's examine a neighborhood for a moment. In this neighborhood, most houses have some type of yard space that is landscaped or decorated according to the owner's individual taste. Can something as simple as one's yard decor be affected by perceptual factors and the perception process? Are socially derived psychological factors influential in this kind of situation?

Let's take a drive through "Pleasant Acres." We are struck by the varied and different landscapes. One yard has been meticulously decorated with religious statues and ornaments. In the middle of the yard is a fountain with a prayer verse inscribed at its base. The owners of this home attend church regularly and are involved in the church choir. The house next door boasts a cactus garden, reminiscent of the southwest, complete with cattle skull and sand. This landscape reminds these people of their yard "back home." The home across the street is totally void of any decorations, not even a tree or flower. These homeowners operate on a thrifty budget and believe that spending money on landscaping would be wasteful and extravagant. The final house at the end of the street is that of four single roommates. Their yard decor includes a neon sign on the front porch pointing the way to the door and various metal stadium signs placed in a whimsical ivy garden as a reminder that these guys are serious about their sports.

What do these yards have in common? Nothing you say. Well, you are somewhat right, but the common element in each of these examples is that the yard decor is a direct result of each individual's social influences. One yard has religious overtones; the cacti represent a cultural value or custom; the yard void of decoration reflects an economic consideration; and the sports theme is a family (roommates are your family for a time) choice. In fact, whether or not we like the various decors might also be determined by our own social influences.

Lifestyle Choices

Our everyday experience and the daily choices we make can directly influence our perceptual processes. When these choices are major decisions in and of themselves, we call them **lifestyle choices**, and they include our career, our group memberships, and even our morals and values. Each of these individual choices has a bearing on what relationships we enter into, where we choose to live, and numerous other decisions we make. These elements also influence us when we are making judgments of others' behaviors. Let's use different perceptions of gambling as an example. A person who has been taught by his parents and religious leaders to view gambling as morally wrong might extend this view to include judging anyone who gambles as morally corrupt. Someone else, say, a member of a sorority, may feel that gambling is perfectly acceptable. In fact, every year she organizes and sells the raffle tickets for the big quilt giveaway and helps with the annual bingo fun night, both of which are forms of gambling. Lifestyle choices and past experiences have led each of these people to perceive the act of gambling in a different light. They have been influenced by, and have made perceptual determinations from, psychological factors.

Cultural Influences

Regardless of the fact that the perception *process* is common to all humans, the outcomes are not always universally shared. As mentioned previously, one of the factors that influence our perceptions is past experiences. Also mentioned previously, past experiences include cultural aspects such as the traditions and values that our parents taught us as children, acceptable behaviors that we learned in school and at home, and the expectations we should have for meaningful relationships. For many of us, the cultural aspects that influence us are based on what is generally accepted as normal in the United States (although, because there are diverse cultures in the U.S., there may be multiple versions of normal). However, cultural differences can exist for people living within the same country, the same region of the country, and even the same neighborhood. Thus, when we talk about cultural influences on our perception, we need to remember that these influences are not the same for everyone.

If, as a child growing up in the United States, children in your family were seen and not heard at the dinner table, your perception of children who constantly chatter during dinner might be different from that of a person who grew up with a free rein to speak whenever they chose during dinner. If you were having dinner with a family who allowed their children to speak and interact freely during dinner, you might perceive these children as annoying and intrusive, while someone else might perceive them as charming and intelligent. That is not to say that your perception is wrong, or the other person's is right. Each is what it is. Nevertheless, culture has influenced each of your perceptions.

Problems, confusion, and misunderstandings arise when cultural influences cause us to make incorrect judgments or assumptions about others or cause us to believe that our perception is the right one, and any other is wrong. Therefore, we need to be aware of and sensitive to differences in cultural influences. Sensitivity to cultural differences and how

---

 Activity for Further Understanding

Perception at Work

Pretend that you work for the student activities organization on your college campus. You have been asked to design a new student center. You must address the following issues:

1. Where will the facility be located on campus? Why?
2. What will the decor be (i.e., color, chairs, tables, TV available, etc.)?
3. What activities will be allowed at the facility?
4. What will be the hours of operation?
5. Who will run the facility?

When you finish answering the above questions, you are to compare your answers with one of your classmate's answers. Why are they different or similar?

1. What physiological factors were at work in your decisions?
2. What psychological factors were at work in your decisions?
3. Whose plan is best? Why?

culture affects perceptions helps us to be more effective communicators. If we try to understand how another person views the world, we will have a better chance of establishing common ground with that person and enjoy a meaningful communication experience.

Characteristics of Perception

We have thus far examined what perception is and the physiological and psychological factors that influence this process. We have looked at several examples in which these factors are apparent.

All of our perceptions are subject to these many influences that result in our interpretations that then guide our behavior. Now we'll look at the characteristics of the perception process itself. Keeping these in mind will help you remember that although perceptions differ, the perception process is the same for all of us.

Perception Is a Selective Process

We select what it is we wish to pay attention to. In other words, when we experience something, we choose what to notice and what to ignore. We see what we want to see, and hear what we want to hear. If you are listening to two people talk about the same situation, you will notice that they don't tell exactly the same story. Even though they were both involved in the exact same situation, they didn't experience it in the same way. This is why eyewitnesses to the same event often give different accounts about it. Two witnesses to an accident may notice different aspects. One witness may have seen three vehicles while another heard a child. Perception is selective because the process is based on choices made by a person due to sensory mode, culture, previous experience, or any of the other factors we discussed earlier.

Perception Is Not Always a Detailed Process

Since any situation can involve numerous details, and perception is a selective process, it is also feasible that we might leave details out when we experience a situation. In other words, we make mistakes because we don't focus on all of the details, and individuals focus on different details. For example, think of the last time you gave directions to someone. Recently I (Mary) gave directions to my house to a friend. I told her to turn right two blocks after the local convenience market. She turned on the wrong street because I actually live three streets from the store. Why did I leave out a street? I honestly did not know it existed! I have lived in this area my whole life. I have traveled the main road thousands of times. Yet, I had never seen that street until my friend told me about it. Even then I had to drive to it myself to verify that it was really there. I left out very important details in giving her directions. The road bordered an elementary school, which was a factor in my perception. I concluded that the reason I didn't notice the street is that being a mother (a social influence), I am so focused on children, school buses, and watching carefully ahead, that I never noticed this very tiny, barely marked dead-end street that is near the school. Yet there it was! I left out this detail, an important one to my friend, who spent time driving around looking for a house that did not exist on the wrong street! Leaving out details can cause ineffective communication, which causes problems. Another problem can occur when we organize details in such a way as to fit the information already stored in our minds. Sometimes this information is wrong. When we judge a situation or a person according to preestablished details or categories stored in our minds, we are creating a **stereotype**. Let's look at an example of this phenomenon.

Pretend you are shopping at the mall and you notice a barefoot child with numerous stains on his overalls. He is holding a pair of torn socks in his hand and his face is filthy with grime and who knows what! What mother would have so little pride as to let her child run around the mall in this state, and unattended? After all, your mother never did! You immediately judge that this child's parent must not be a fit mother. Your perception is already being influenced by the social psychological factor of family background. You turn away in disgust, vowing never to let your children look this way in public if and when you have any.

What you did not select to pay attention to (perceive) were the details surrounding the boy. If you had, you may have noticed a young mother nearby with a newborn baby, packing a diaper bag in an attempt to leave the local hamburger joint. Her hands are full and she is telling another young mom what a terrible experience they had. First, her son spilled his ketchup down the front of his new overalls. Then he took his shoes off and caught his socks on a chair, ripping a hole in one of them. After his shoes were back on, he ran out of the restaurant to play outside. It was muddy outside, and he managed to transfer all of the mud and dirt from his shoes to his clothes. He then decided to take his shoes off again and leave the restaurant without mom, his shoes, or his baby sister. Mom vowed to take him home and give him a good bath with lots of soap just as soon as she could catch him! She doesn't seem like an unfit mother now, does she? You selected what was obvious to you and made a perceptual mistake. You then proceeded to place the label of "unfit" on this mother. You did so because the circumstances you chose to pay attention to fit your criteria (stereotype) of unfit mothers. In actuality, this little boy was wearing the "battle scars" of a very happy playtime! What we perceive is a combination of what is and what we think it is.

Challenges to the Perception Process

If you have learned anything from this chapter, hopefully it is that people do not perceive the world in exactly the same way. Forgetting this can cause problems in your communication with others. How many times have you gone to a barber or beautician and told him to take "just a little off the top," "trim it a bit," or "leave the length and just take some off the sides"? Then you leave the salon. When you get home and look in the mirror, you can't see a difference in your hair and feel like you have wasted your money, or you think way too much hair was cut and you feel scalped. Why did this happen? Couldn't the barber understand simple English? You said "a little." Think about Jason and Susan. Jason said he was going out for "a little while." When he returned two hours later he thought that's what he had done. Susan, on the other hand, considered "a little while" to be a much shorter period of time. This type of misunderstanding is caused by different connotations of the word "little." Unfortunately, discovering these differences in meaning occurred after the deed was already done, but both of these cases demonstrate the importance of being precise. Checking the other person's perception of "reality" and what you consider "reality" is very important for effective communication and presents a challenge to the process.

We Organize and Interpret Information Differently

How many times have you been asked to participate in a survey where you have been invited to give your views on a new product or service offered by a company? You may have been provided with a form on which to record your opinions. The form included a scale to measure your satisfaction. The number one on the scale indicated that you were very dissatisfied with the product, and the number five indicated that you were very satisfied with the product. The scale further used the number three as a midpoint to indicate that you are neutral about the product, or have no opinion whatsoever. These scales, known as Likert Scales, are designed to measure consumer "likes" or satisfaction about a particular good or service.

Let's examine this example further. We (Tracey and Mary) try a new beef sandwich at the local fast-food restaurant, and both of us fill out a survey indicating how well we like the sandwich. Tracey likes it very much and would buy it again. She likes beef in general, and this particular restaurant is close to her house. Considering the cost, taste, and convenience, she gives the sandwich a rating of five, very satisfied with the beef sandwich. Mary, on the other hand, likes the sandwich, but she thinks the portion is too small. She is also a salad, bread, and potato lover and will often forego meat with her meal. She wouldn't go out of her way to buy it again. The restaurant is not one of her favorites, and her husband does the cooking, so she doesn't have to be worry about convenience. Although she doesn't have much interest in the sandwich and doesn't care if it's available for future purchase, she likes the taste. Like Tracey, she also rates the sandwich five, very satisfied. Now, what has the restaurant learned about their customers' satisfaction with the sandwich? Do they have an accurate understanding of each customer's perception? If the restaurant owners assume that all customers who give the sandwich a rating of five are very satisfied and will buy it again, they have made a big mistake! Some customers who gave it a rating of five, like Mary, may have no intention of buying it again. Without examining the explanations (interpretations) behind the answers, the restaurant does not have an accurate indication of how popular the sandwich will be. Truly understanding each other's perceptions must involve more than focusing on the outcome. It must include knowledge of the perception process—that is, the behind-the-scenes process of organizing, interpreting, and evaluating the information, all areas of considerable challenge.

We know that our personal environments develop and change over time due to our own experiences. When Tracey was packing to move to a new house, one of the items stacked to go in the moving van was an old beat up suitcase with pictures of The Beatles glued all over it. Her husband looked at it and casually said, "We don't need to take that old thing." Her reaction was much different than he expected. She became furious and let him know that it was going with them! He was completely taken aback and let the matter drop. You see, in that suitcase was all of her Beatle memorabilia, magazines, Beatle dolls, and the tickets and program from when she'd actually seen them in person many years before. It represented a simple, happy time in her life, and even though she never really looked at the contents, it was of great value to her due to the memories it represented. To her husband it was just junk.

There's a follow-up to this story that illustrates how our interpretations can change when we are exposed to new information. Several months after the move, Tracey's husband came home from work and asked, "Do you have Beatle dolls in that old suitcase in the attic"? She replied she had all four of them in perfect condition in the original packaging. His eyes got wide and he said, "Do you know how much money those are worth?" That old "worthless" suitcase now had value to him since he had learned how much money the contents were worth. While both perceived the suitcase as valuable, their perceptions of why it was valuable were quite different!

These differences in perception occur with alarming frequency because we fail to remember that something may mean far more to someone else, and for different reasons, than it does to us. Because none of us have exactly the same personal environments, none of us will perceive information in exactly the same way. There are many influences at work in the perception process. These influences are constantly creating a "map" with which we navigate the world, and as most of us know, reading a map can be quite challenging!

Decreasing Perceptual Misunderstandings

It is impossible for everyone's perceptions to be the same, so we need to be able to send clear messages. To do this we need to be aware of the different factors that mold and influence our perceptions and come to understandings about our perceptions.

Maybe you are wondering how we can agree on anything when we see things so differently. Agreements are possible, and shared perceptions can and do occur. When a difference of opinion occurs, or when it is hard to understand another person's viewpoint, take a moment to analyze the cause of the disagreement. Is it a case of misunderstanding, a lack of information (see chapter 1) or is it a case of physiological or psychological perception at work? If differences in perception are the problem, the following communication skills can help you penetrate perceptual barriers.

1. *Listen to what the other person is really saying.* Don't just listen to the words but also listen to how they are said. Notice any other signals, such as facial expressions or body movements. Use all of your senses to listen, not just your eyes.

2. *Be thorough as you try to understand the other person.* What is the environment, culture, family background, or sensory mode of this person? Use your imagination to creatively transport yourself into their shoes (empathy). Explore every possible scenario.

3. *Make a firm decision to withhold your own perceptions.* It won't be easy trying to withhold your own perceptions, but only through such a commitment will the rewards of effective communication be achieved. You can't understand another viewpoint if you are stuck in yours.

4. *Agree to disagree.* If after you have completed the first three suggestions you cannot come to a consensus, don't. I know this sounds silly, but let the other person know you respect his view. Be clear about your own view. Do not be defensive but be comfortable that the other person is okay and so are you. This is how we get past the "I'm right, you're wrong" argument that so frequently results in communication breakdowns.

Conclusion

Perception is the act of becoming aware of information. This process is influenced by physiological and psychological factors. Because of the uniqueness of each individual, the perception process is not always accurate. We select what we want to pay attention to and often leave out important details. Sometimes we focus on the most negative aspect of a situation and, therefore, perceive information inaccurately. Sometimes we are unwilling to change our opinions. It is important to realize that this process is a selective one. In order to be effective communicators it is necessary to step back from the process once in a while and ask yourself what you are "really" experiencing. We can manage the perception process by using all of our senses to be empathetic. Our goal should be to reach agreements when possible through open communication. When agreement seems impossible due to vast perceptual differences, the best course of action is agreeing to disagree. It is not ultimately who is right or wrong, the goal is to communicate. This is a key to our survival.

DISCUSSION QUESTIONS

1. Discuss a situation that you have been in where a difference of opinion or misunderstanding existed due to physiological factors.

2. Discuss a situation that you have been in where a difference of opinion or misunderstanding existed due to psychological factors.

3. How will understanding another person's perceptual influences help you to be a more effective communicator?

4. Perception is selective. Discuss a time when your selective perception has led to a misunderstanding.

5. Explain the phrase, "One man's trash is another man's treasure" using the characteristics of perception presented in this chapter.

KEY TERMS

lifestyle choices
perception
physiological factors

psychological factors
social situations
stereotype

chapter nine

Defensiveness

Just Leave Me Alone!

CHAPTER HIGHLIGHTS

- When we are perceived negatively, we are compelled to defend ourselves.
- We have two selves that we attempt to protect.
- Our perceived self is what we believe to be true about our self.
- Our presenting self is what we show others and want them to believe.
- When we are attacked, we feel defensive and want to protect our "selves."
- We use fight mechanisms to defend ourselves.
- We use flee mechanisms to defend ourselves.
- The emotional tone of our relationships determines our communication climate.
- A negative climate can cause defense-producing behaviors.
- A positive climate can cause defense-eliminating, or supportive, behaviors.
- Gibb categories can help us identify these behaviors and avoid defensiveness.
- You can become a more effective communicator if you eliminate defensiveness.

Susan hated the end of the month. It was the time when she and Jason would sit down at the kitchen table and balance the checkbook. For hours, they would examine each entry in the checkbook. It was not that money was exceptionally tight, and the checkbook balance always agreed with the bank statement, it was that Jason was a perfectionist. Since Susan was the one who would stop by after work to pick up a few items here and there, she was responsible for most of the entries in the checkbook. Whenever they balanced the checkbook together, Jason would question her about each entry, asking her what items she bought for the total recorded in the check register. She could not always remember every detail, and she thought it was unfair for Jason to imply that she was irresponsible for not remembering. Jason would question why laundry soap cost so much or why she bought toilet paper three times last month. Susan did not believe she was irresponsible or extravagant. After all, when you needed toilet paper, you didn't worry about how many times this month you had already bought some. You just bought more. When Jason questioned her, she felt he was attacking her budgeting skills. It made her feel very defensive. She felt like she had to constantly justify and defend her actions. She hated balancing the checkbook.

Jason couldn't understand why Susan didn't keep better track of how she spent their money. They went through the same routine every month. He would question her, she would not know the answers, and then she would pout. This problem occurred monthly. Jason found it frustrating. It should be easy to sit down and balance the checkbook. Jason had watched his parents do this same thing every month. His mother would have a list of every single item that she had purchased so that when his father had a question about something, she had an answer. It had all seemed very simple. Jason liked details. He liked to know where every cent of their budget was being spent. He could not understand why Susan wasn't the same way. He also couldn't understand why the checkbook was such a struggle every month. Why did she get so touchy when he asked her such simple questions about where she had spent their money? Jason hated balancing the checkbook.

What Is Defensiveness?

When we are involved in a misunderstanding or an argument, it is natural for us to feel uncomfortable and insecure. If others do not react to us in the way that we expect them to, we may feel compelled to defend our opinion or ourselves. If others perceive us negatively, we may fight back in order to avoid harm. In previous chapters, we have discussed how important self-concept, gender, and perception are in effective communication. If we experience problems in our communications with others due to any of these influences, we may feel misunderstood or misjudged. These feelings can cause us to feel defensive. Defensiveness is one of the most damaging elements to effective communication.

Each of us has two selves that we may feel the need to defend from attacks by others. The **perceived self** is what we honestly believe to be true about our self, while our **presenting self** is what we show to others and want them to believe is true; it is our "public" self. This is not to imply that we are two-faced or have a split personality. In fact, for some of us, these two selves may not be that much different. However, we do tend to consciously control the self we show to others.

You may wish to be hired for a job, impress your peers, or be accepted by a particular group. To accomplish these goals, you may modify or totally change aspects of your behavior when around others in these situations. Often we have personal beliefs, experiences, or attributes that we would rather not disclose. Furthermore, we may limit or control what we show to strangers compared to what we show to people with whom we interact on a regular basis.

You may interact quite differently with strangers at a party than you would with your friends. You may talk and act differently with friends than you would with your grandparents. Friends who may be your same age, and share similar interests and activities, are more likely to share your feelings and opinions as well. You feel comfortable that your friends will accept these feelings and not judge you negatively. They probably share many of them with you. Your grandparents, on the other hand, may not share your taste in music or social activities, let alone your views and opinions! The self you "present" to them is likely very different from the one you show to your friends. You may be on your best behavior when you are with your grandparents. You may attend church rather than go bungee jumping, and eat roast beef instead of tacos. You may discuss Christmas and school, but not the party you attended last night!

Many of the concepts we hold in our private self are the same as those we show the world in our presenting self. However, those that are contradictory often can cause the largest and most intense displays of defensiveness. **Defensiveness** is defined as the feeling we get that causes us to take actions to protect our presenting self. If I know that my coworkers see me as a responsible person, and yet privately I know that I tend to shirk my duties if I can slide by, I will become defensive if my responsibility is questioned. It is as if the person accusing me of being irresponsible has seen through my public façade and seen the real me. She has caught me in the act of betraying my private self in public.

Defensiveness is one of the biggest barriers to communication that we face. It is detrimental to communication because it is usually recipro- cal. **Reciprocal defensiveness** means that when one person becomes defensive during a conversation with another person, the other person is likely to respond in a defensive manner as well. Once all the participants are trying to defend their presenting selves, the likelihood of any honest communication occurring is remote. Once we begin defending ourselves, we tend to be so consumed with the process that we fail to communicate.

Defense Mechanisms

Defensiveness occurs because we feel threatened. In that respect, we can say this is the only singular characteristic of defensiveness. Yet once the attack is perceived, an emotional response will occur. When we are physically attacked, we have two options in defending ourselves: We can fight the attacker and try to overcome him, or we can flee the attacker in an attempt to avoid being hurt. The same options are available when you believe your presenting self has been attacked. These choices as to whether or not we fight or flee are called **defense mechanisms**. These are behaviors or reactions we display when we are under attack.

Fight Mechanisms

We use **fight mechanisms** to defend our public image, usually from a verbal accusation. One of the most often-used fight mechanisms is **rationalization**. For example, if our friend accuses us of being self-centered because we promised to phone him to talk over a problem he had, but didn't do it, we might rationalize not doing it by saying, "I didn't call you like I said I would because the kids were sick." We hope our (untrue) reason will convince our friend (the attacker) to reverse his opinion of us. The rationalization defense often has the advantage of not causing reciprocal defensiveness. Our attacker is unaware that even though the kids were sick, we could have found time to make the call, so he accepts our "rational" explanation.

Another frequently used fight mechanism is **sarcasm**. Paralanguage (see chapter 2) is the distinguishing attack feature of sarcasm. The words spoken may mean one thing, but the tone of voice and the emphasis on specific words make the real meaning of the message entirely different: Your friend has just arrived 45 minutes late for your meeting, you greet her by saying, "This is a *wonderful* way to get started." You obviously don't mean "wonderful" in its typical sense; in fact the way you say it, sarcastically, makes it mean the exact opposite.

A third type of fight mechanism is **projection,** where we bounce or "project" the attack back onto our attacker. "Sure the house is a mess, but when was the last time *you* did the dishes?" With this tact, we hope to distract his focus on us by pointing out he is just as guilty.

Verbal aggression is another fight mechanism we use when we become defensive. Basically, we use a loud voice to "drown" out our attacker's comments. The philosophy seems to be, "He who yells loudest, wins."

Flee Mechanisms

Flee mechanisms are used when we choose not to confront our attacker but choose to run away as a means of defense. We may choose to avoid conflict for any number of reasons. Whatever our reason for fleeing, we have several flight mechanisms that we use. With certain situations, we can use **displacement.** For example, our boss tells us we aren't doing a good job. We don't want to rationalize, use sarcasm, or fight with the boss, so instead we avoid the boss and go home and yell or kick the door at a later time.

We may use **compensation** as a defense. With this method we change the subject or bring up another topic. Therefore we compensate by talking about something that we are knowledgeable about and can discuss with more success. "Yeah, I may have flunked math, but I got an A in English." Another flee mechanism is reacting as if nothing has happened by using **apathy**, pretending we have no feeling on the subject—acting like we don't care—the opposite of how we really feel. "Okay, so he stood me up. Big deal! I don't care anyway."

We may even try to avoid the situation physically by using **retreat**. We can walk out of the room, become engrossed in a TV show, start working on our computer, or "retreat" to some other activity, ignoring the other person completely. Different than a physical retreat, is a mental retreat. This allows us to enter into our own thoughts or daydreams where we are in control of the situation. This defense mechanism is known as **fantasy**. Here we try to convince ourselves that what we have been accused of isn't true.

We might offer excuses by retorting that the accusation is inaccurate. This is another defense mechanism called **repression**. Repression allows us to avoid an attack by pretending the action didn't take place or by disavowing any connection to it: "You must be mistaken about that; my children would never spray paint the side of your garage!"

Sometimes, to avoid a confrontation, we choose to revert to a time when we were incapable of being responsible because of our age or size. This mechanism is known as **regression**. When you tell your mother it's not that you don't want to help her with the laundry, but rather, you are afraid you will ruin the clothes due to your ineptness, you are using a form of regression. You know you are perfectly capable of washing a load of clothes, but act like a child and pretend you don't know how. You regress to the carefree days of childhood.

Finally, there is the flee mechanism of **reversal**. Rather than admit we failed to do something, or did something we shouldn't have, we defend ourselves by trying to reverse the other person's perception. We bypass any discussion with them but do something like sending flowers, making a favorite dinner, or buying the kids another toy.

All of these actions are common ways we try to protect our presenting selves, our public images. Which defense mechanism or which combination of them we use depends upon a number of factors. Primarily, we choose the defense mechanism that we believe will be the most successful in protecting our public image. We quickly calculate the attack, the relationship involved, the environment, and the consequences of the encounter. The result determines whether we believe we should fight or flee. In other instances we simply use the defense mechanism we have found useful in the past. Chances are that these methods are not unfamiliar to you. You probably can remember times when you used each one. In fact, we used instances of our own past defensive behaviors as examples for each one!

Understand that defensiveness is not necessarily negative. There is nothing inherently wrong or necessarily bad about needing to protect yourself. It is a natural behavior that all people use when they feel threatened. However, being defensive without being willing to examine why results in ineffective communication. Becoming defensive often prolongs a disagreement. Failure to examine why we are defensive can lead to ineffective intrapersonal communication as well. If we become defensive, we often ignore the voice in our head, which can help us to identify the real issue. Were you misunderstood by your attacker? Is there any truth to the accusation that you may need to examine? Finally, if we are repeatedly defensive, the result will be reciprocal defensiveness from others. When you are perceived as being a defensive person, other people often feel uncomfortable sharing their views and opinions with you and will begin to avoid you. If communicating with others is important to you, then becoming defensive can complicate this goal.

Defense-Producing and Defense-Eliminating Behaviors

What Causes Defensiveness?

We become defensive because we perceive we are being attacked. As we have learned, we have no control over the actions of others. Therefore, no one can guarantee that we will never have our public image threatened. People say and do hurtful things that can cause us to feel offended. The emotional tone of our relationships creates a **climate** or environment in which we attempt to communicate. If this communication climate is stressful, negative, or threatening, we will become defensive. Often the communication climate is significantly influenced by the behavior of one or more persons. Psychologist Jack Gibb categorized six behaviors that cause people to become defensive. These behaviors are known as **defense-producing behaviors**. Not only do they cause defensiveness, but they contribute to a negative communication climate as well. Let's examine these six behaviors in more detail.

1. *Evaluation.* When we evaluate someone or something, we are passing judgment; we say something or someone is right, wrong, stupid, intelligent, messy, or clean. Even if our role as a parent, teacher, or boss warrants our use of evaluation, the person being evaluated will likely respond with a defensive reaction. Evaluation produces defensiveness because it uses *you messages*, such as you should have done better, you make me mad, or you are lazy. These statements point to the other person as being totally responsible for our inferences to his actions or character. We state them as if they are fact, therefore passing judgment on them.

2. *Control.* Anytime we attempt to control a situation, we create a defensive climate. When we act like the boss by telling others what to do, we not only negate their abilities, we also take away their desire to accomplish a goal on their own. When we place ourselves in a position of authority, even when we have the right to do so, we contribute to feelings of defensiveness in others. We have set up a

game in which we have declared ourselves the player with the power. This will usually result in our "opponent" putting up a fight.

3. *Strategy.* When we try to manipulate others into doing what we want we are using strategy. This may achieve our goal of getting to the movie on Saturday night, but the chances of the person we have manipulated having a good time are slim. He will probably be defensive and angry because he was tricked into doing something he did not want to do. If a person allows himself to be manipulated, he often gets angry or resentful.

4. *Neutrality.* We engage in neutrality when we fail to respond to someone who is trying to engage us in conversation. Even if done unintentionally we send the message that we are not interested in what that person has to say. An environment in which a person feels ignored is ripe for problems. If my spouse comes home from work and wants to discuss a problem he is having with a coworker, and I ignore him by flipping through the television channels, he will become defensive. He will transfer his initial anger at the coworker and add it to his anger at me. Then he will let all of it spill forth, because he felt ignored.

5. *Superiority.* Acting as if we are better than someone else, for whatever reason, is the defense-producing behavior of superiority. This behavior implies that because we have more knowledge, more authority, or more money, we are better than others in some way. Acting "better than thou" creates a climate where defensiveness will most likely be reciprocated. Nothing will be accomplished. If a teacher treats students with disdain because she believes she is superior, the class will be defensive and most likely unreceptive to any attempts made by her to engage them in the learning process. Having an advanced academic degree does not make the teacher better than the students. The teacher is just more knowledgeable in a particular subject area. Holding a position of authority, for whatever reason, does not make us superior.

6. *Certainty.* If you know someone who is always right, no matter what proof you give to the contrary, then you are familiar with the defense-producing behavior of certainty. People who act with certainty believe there are only two ways to look at things, their way, which is the right way, or everyone else's way, which is the wrong way. These people engage in behavior that causes us to feel that everything we say will be attacked. These people produce defensiveness whenever they interact with others.

What Eliminates Defensiveness?

If we become defensive because we perceive we are under attack, then it stands to reason that if we felt no threat we would not become defensive. How can we, as effective communicators, avoid making others feel defensive? We can attempt to create a communication climate in which the emotional tone of the relationship is positive, calming, and supportive. We can send a message to others that we care about them and acknowledge that they may have opinions that differ from ours. Gibb categorized six behaviors that send a message of support and acceptance. These behaviors are known as **supportive behaviors**. Let's examine these in detail.

1. *Description.* When we state our thoughts and feelings for what they are, our opinion, we are engaging in **description**. Describing our feelings results in more honest communication. Saying that someone's actions affect us by using "I" messages is much less defense producing than using evaluative "you" messages. I messages do not damage the self-esteem of the other person involved because they are stated as our opinion, not fact. For example, saying, "I feel unloved," or "I am upset about my curfew," are statements that reflect our own thoughts and do not evaluate others.

2. *Problem Orientation.* When we use the supportive behavior of problem orientation, we take into account the other person's feelings and ideas, and incorporate them as part of our solution. It is a process that involves cooperation. With this approach, when a problem is seen to exist, all parties define what they perceive as the problem. They then try to reach a mutual consensus on how to solve the problem. This takes time, but in the end it works better than trying to be in control.

3. *Spontaneity.* When we honestly and directly say what we think or want on the spur of the moment, we are engaging in spontaneity. For example, "I left my assignment at home, can I bring it next class period?" In this case, the instructor has the opportunity to answer the student based on real facts and honest information. It is more effective to tell someone what we really want than try to manipulate her. This method does not always result in getting what we desire, but it does help eliminate any defensiveness in the person we are communicating with because we have not engaged in manipulation.

4. *Empathy.* The ability to put yourself in someone else's place is called empathy. This is one of the most useful skills you can learn to use as a communicator. Empathy is the ability to understand the words, actions, feelings, thoughts, and personal environment of the speaker. You attempt to put yourself in that person's place to understand how she is feeling. This skill does not require you to agree with the other person; you are just trying to experience a situation from her viewpoint. When my spouse comes home from work and wants me to listen when he talks about coworker problems, I don't have to agree with him or attempt to solve his prob-

lem. If I listen and show I care, I am empathizing (see chapter 4 for a discussion of empathic listening).

5. *Equality.* The supportive behavior of promoting equality in our relationships can produce positive results. Treating others as equals does not negate the fact that some people have more knowledge or skill in certain areas than others. What equality does do is show respect for differences we possess as unique individuals. Our students are perfectly willing to concede that we probably know a bit more about communication than they do, but we know there are an infinite number of things they are more knowledgeable about as well. We all possess abilities that, while different, are not necessarily unequal. Apples and oranges aren't the same, but they are equally good fruits!

6. *Provisionalism.* This supportive behavior can be used to lessen defensiveness by allowing another person to state his beliefs, opinions, and feelings. Provisionalism does not require a consensus, and should be used when you *have* to be in charge. This occurs when you and you alone will be responsible for the outcome. Listening and attempting to incorporate some of the other person's ideas into the plan can lessen the likelihood of defensiveness, even if his ideas may not be able to be incorporated into your solution. The fact that the person has been allowed to state them will make the atmosphere less hostile and solutions more readily accepted.

In summary, having a good understanding of the Gibb defense-producing and defense-eliminating behaviors will help you become a more effective communicator. You are now aware of those behaviors that can create a defensive climate and should avoid using them. How a person interprets a situation is what makes it defense producing. Your intent may not be to cause defensiveness in another person, but if she thinks otherwise, you have a defensive climate on your hands. It is equally important that you are able to recognize these behaviors in others. While we can't create a totally nondefensive climate, we can attempt to set up an environment in which defensiveness is less likely to happen. The Gibb behavioral categories can help you recognize when a defense-producing behavior has occurred. That way you can initiate a supportive behavior to establish a positive climate in which effective communication can happen. The chart on the following page can help you know which supportive behavior to use when you are confronted with someone reacting defensively.

To use the Gibb method of eliminating defensiveness, try to identify which behavior is being exhibited in the defense-producing list. Then attempt to employ the corresponding supportive behavior in the right column. For example, if your friend thinks you have ignored her when she was trying to talk to you, you have been using neutrality. She has

Gibb Behavioral Categories

Defense Producing		*Defense Eliminating (supportive)*
1. Evaluation	use	Description
2. Control	use	Problem Orientation
3. Strategy	use	Spontaneity
4. Neutrality	use	Empathy
5. Superiority	use	Equality
6. Certainty	use	Provisionalism

The Gibb Categories of Defensive and Supportive Behaviors from "Defensive Communication" by Jack R. Gibb published in the *Journal of Communication*, Vol. 11:3 (1961). Reprinted with permission of Blackwell Publishing.

become defensive in response to this behavior. Try using empathy with her; listen and put yourself in her situation: how would you feel if she ignored you? Using the Gibb method does not always insure success, but it usually results in eliminating reciprocal defensiveness or keeps a problem from escalating. This opens up the door for more effective problem solving. Finally, remember that avoiding use of the defense-producing behaviors in your own actions creates a more positive communication climate from the start.

  ## Activity for Further Understanding

Defensiveness and You

Write about a time you became defensive with another person.

• Describe the situation.

• Identify the defense-producing behavior exhibited by the person you were communicating with that caused you to become defensive.

• Identify the fight or flee mechanism you used to resolve the problem.

• Describe the outcome.

• Discuss how the outcome might have changed if you had used the corresponding Gibb defense eliminating (supportive) behavior instead of fighting or fleeing.

Now that you have completed the activity, do you find that there are certain defense producing behaviors that cause you to become defensive more often? Which defense mechanisms do you typically use? Do you think the Gibb method is an effective way to eliminate defensiveness? Why or why not? Justify your response.

Conclusion

Defensiveness is a normal reaction to comments or situations that we perceive as an attack on our presenting self. Everyone has at one time or another experienced this behavior. Defensiveness is not bad, nor is it undesirable, but for communication to be effective, defensiveness must be kept at a minimum. The next time you find yourself becoming defensive, stop and think about what fight or flee mechanism you are really using. Try to apply the Gibb defense-eliminating (supportive) behavior to the situation. You'll be surprised at how this key can unlock the door to a more positive communication climate.

DISCUSSION QUESTIONS

1. Which of the Gibb defense-producing behaviors affect you the most when used by others? Why do you think they affect you in this way?

2. Who puts you in a defensive mode most of the time? Why do you believe this happens so frequently?

3. What part of your presenting self do you tend to defend the most often? Why?

4. What fight mechanisms do you use? Give an example of why you believe this to be true.

5. What flee mechanisms do you use? Give an example of why you believe this to be true.

KEY TERMS

apathy
certainty
climate
compensation
control
defense mechanism
defense-producing behaviors
defensiveness
description
displacement
empathy
equality
evaluation
fantasy
fight mechanisms
flee mechanisms
neutrality

perceived self
presenting self
problem orientation
projection
provisionalism
rationalization
reciprocal defensiveness
regression
repression
retreat
reversal
sarcasm
spontaneity
strategy
superiority
supportive behaviors
verbal aggression

chapter ten

Conflict

Take a stand, or stand and take it?

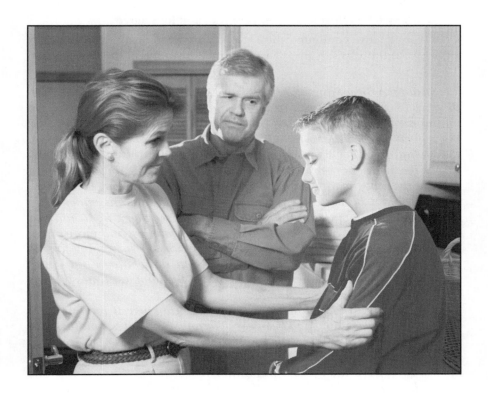

CHAPTER HIGHLIGHTS

- Conflict is natural and unavoidable.
- Gender and culture influence conflict.
- All conflict shares three characteristics: it must be mutually agreed upon, it involves contradictory views, and it involves inconsistent goals.
- There are five ways that we deal with conflict. These ways are known as conflict styles.
- The five conflict styles are: direct aggression, concealed aggression, passiveness, non-assertion, and assertion.
- What conflict style we use depends on our personality and the situation.
- There are several ways to attempt to resolve conflict: I win, you lose; we both lose; let's compromise; and let's agree.
- For effective communication it is important to resolve conflicts.

Susan was becoming more and more anxious every day. As the wedding drew nearer it seemed as if she and Jason grew further apart. No matter what they talked about, it ended up in an argument. They had not agreed on the date or time for the wedding. They had not agreed on the invitations. They had not agreed on the flowers, the church, the colors, or the menu for the reception. In fact, the only thing they had agreed on was that they wanted to be married! It didn't help that her mother and sister had become so involved in the wedding plans either. They would give their opinion, and Jason would get so angry, he would just walk away. He had been leaving to go to the gym more and more often. The last time she had asked him for his opinion on something for the wedding, he had said, "Ask your mother, and do whatever she says." What a mess! This was supposed to be one of the happiest times of their lives and everybody was miserable!

Jason had just blown up at Susan again. He knew it really wasn't her fault that everything had been going wrong. He liked her mother and sister, but he did not like their ideas for the wedding. He had tried to give his opinion, but they had looked at him as if he had just sprouted horns. They were always breathing down his and Susan's necks. His future in-laws had been over at the condo every night for the last two weeks. He needed some space. He was ready to tell Susan he thought they should elope. Why couldn't they come up with an easy solution to this wedding mess? He was becoming very angry because Susan's family was trying to control their lives.

What Is Conflict?

For most people conflict means diminished happiness. Conflicts arise due to many reasons: money, sex, power, time, and wedding plans. As you may have noticed, Jason is the recipient of the defense-producing behavior of control exhibited by Susan's mother and sister. As we learned in the last chapter, using the Gibb defense-eliminating strategies cannot always guarantee that a positive communication climate will occur. When Susan's family became controlling, Jason had attempted to use the supportive behavior of problem orientation, but it had not worked. Even the most prudent use of support cannot guarantee that conflicts will not occur. Some people are not receptive to these supportive behaviors, as Jason found out with Susan's mother and sister. We may dream about an easy solution, as Jason is doing, and we may wish for a life without arguments, but this is just not feasible.

If you could wave a magic wand and remove all conflict from your life, would you? Before you attempt to answer this question, think for a moment about what conflict can add to your life. Think of the excitement of a baseball game. One team is trying to score runs, while the other team attempts to stop them from reaching this goal. If you are an athlete, recall the satisfaction of competition. As a student, think of the struggle to complete your term paper on time and how you felt when it was finally finished. The conflicts that we experience are not inherently bad, nor are the results of conflict necessarily negative. As you will recall from the chapter on perception, no two people perceive things in exactly the same way. It is inevitable that disagreements will arise and conflicts occur. The problem with conflict is that most of the time it turns into a power struggle that ends in both parties becoming defensive. However, when we use effective communication as a means to resolve conflict, it can actually strengthen relationships. The result is satisfaction and a sense of accomplishment. Besides, conflict is unavoidable and therefore learning how to deal with it effectively is a necessary key in learning to survive.

Conflict is a struggle over something, whether it is significant others disagreeing about what to have for supper or neighbors disagreeing over a property boundary. Most of the conflicts we face in our lives fall somewhere in between these two extremes. We quarrel with our roommate over whose turn it is to do the dishes or with our spouse over the budget. We challenge our parents about curfew or argue with them about keeping our room clean. We question a teacher about a grade. These are conflicts that we must resolve. Even though any issue or topic can result in conflict, there are two primary factors that contribute significantly to conflicts and a struggle for power or control.

What Contributes to Conflict?

There are two factors that have been shown to contribute to conflict: gender and culture. Throughout our study of interpersonal communication in this text, we have seen that these two influences play a significant role in our communication effectiveness. Their role in how effective we are at resolving conflict is no exception. How we handle conflict is impacted by whether we are male or female and by the environment in which we were raised.

Gender

Men and women behave differently, as we have learned. Whether you are a supporter of the nature argument or the nurture argument makes no difference. We do know that, due to hormones, men usually react more aggressively than women do. From the time they are very small, boys are socialized to play rough, be demanding, and be in control of situations. Even organized sports teams support these behaviors. Think of the behavior exhibited on the football field or at a hockey game. Girls, on the other hand, are encouraged to "explore" the world and to experiment with various situations and develop proposals for action. Even when playing house, little girls will exhibit this multivaried approach. Should they feed the baby, cook the dinner, or clean the house first? Should the baby be fed, diapered, and bathed before it is put down for a nap? They use language like should, let's, and maybe. These differences between boys and girls do not change during the aging process. Males attempt to resolve problems through power or control, much like the behaviors used to win a game. The one with power ultimately wins. On the other hand, females attempt to offer several strategic solutions to a problem and "try on" each one before making a decision. These differences affect how the sexes resolve conflicts, with men being concerned about "controlling" an issue, and women wanting to "compromise." This can lead to a woman giving in to a man's demands in order to have harmony in a relationship.

Culture

Culture also has an impact on how we manage conflict. We know that most of us in the United States are taught to be self-sufficient and self-reliant. Although this may seem like a positive quality, when conflicts arise, these qualities can escalate into selfishness. For example, two parties who have complete confidence in their ability to make decisions must resolve a conflict over where a new community center should be built. Each party has personal reasons for wanting it built in the differing locations, and their preferences and reasons are not the same. In order to resolve this conflict, both parties must feel that their needs have been addressed and met. If the parties are intent on satisfying only their own goals, the conflict won't be resolved and the community center won't be built. If you are concerned about your own happiness, you cannot be focused on someone else's. This is the primary difference between an individualistic view and a collectivist view. In a collectivist society the focus is not on the individual but on an entire group. In this type of society, the good of the group as a whole is the ultimate goal. Therefore, the needs of individuals would be put aside to do what is best for the entire community. Most of us have been raised to think independently, and this often accounts for these types of conflicts.

Characteristics of Conflict

Effective communicators have learned that conflict is natural and sometimes unavoidable. Therefore, it must be managed. The first step in managing any conflict is being able to recognize the characteristics of conflict: realizing that a mutually agreed-upon problem exists, that both parties have contradicting views, and that the parties have inconsistent goals.

Mutually Agreed-Upon Problem

You may be thinking that this first characteristic is obvious. However, how many times in the past have you been upset with someone who was unaware that you were upset with her? How many times have you given a person dirty looks or the cold shoulder to show you were annoyed, and she wasn't even aware you were angry? You may think these are examples of conflict, but until the other person understands and is made aware of the conflict, there isn't one. You may lose sleep, get a tension headache, or experience indigestion because of a problem you have with someone else, but until that person is also aware of the problem, it isn't a conflict. Conflict must be recognized and its existence mutually accepted.

Conflicts cause an emotional response. When we are in conflict, we are surrounded by the emotional responses being experienced by all parties involved. Many conflicts start with someone attempting to protect himself from an attack. This perceived attack results in his becoming defensive, as we learned in chapter 9. The defensiveness becomes reciprocal. Once both parties have become aware of one another's defensive behavior, conflict is present. The parties mutually agree that there is an issue or problem.

Contradicting Views

When we are involved in a conflict, our hearts beat faster, we sweat, and our voices become raised. These are all indicators that we are experiencing an emotional response. This type of situation can cause us to be

frustrated, angry, hurt, or humiliated, none of which is conducive to finding a reasonable solution to the problem at hand. One of the reasons we
become so emotional is that we have a personal stake in the outcome of
the conflict. We identify so strongly with the problem that we find it difficult to be rational or objective. Let's say your mother "attacks" you for
being thoughtless. She says, "You were really rude when you didn't call to
say you would be late for dinner." She has made a specific accusation, but
along with it, you feel that she has criticized your personality. You don't
consider yourself to be a thoughtless person. In fact, you view yourself as
a good person who looks out for the well-being of her friends and family
members. Your mother's contradicting opinion of you is hurtful and you
become defensive. This evokes an emotional response, and you feel the
need to defend yourself by speaking up and giving an explanation of why
you aren't thoughtless to correct your mother's negative perception. This
may result in a power struggle with each of you attempting to assert your
opinion in an attempt to gain control of the situation. The chances of
finding a mutually satisfactory resolution are diminished due to the emotional reactions involved and the struggle for control of the conversation.
Often a power struggle ends with one party gaining control, or "winning," and the other party losing. The winner attempts to implement her
own solution to the problem. While this may provide a quick fix for the
immediate conflict, it does not mean the conflict is solved. Conflict exists
between two people and must be mutually agreed upon, as does its solution, for it to be resolved.

Inconsistent Goals

All of us have goals, wants, needs, and desires. We learned in chapter
1 that these needs often guide our communication behavior. The same is
true when a conflict arises. People often perceive that if their goals have
not been met, it is because something or someone is in the way. When we
are prevented from accomplishing our goals by some perceived obstacle,
we attempt to remove it from our path. If you would like to take money
out of your joint savings account and spend it on a new coffee table, but
your spouse wants to buy a new barbeque grill, you are prevented from
accomplishing your goal. Your spouse's "BBQ" is in your way! Each of you
perceives the other as the obstacle in your path to accomplishing your
goal. There may be a solution, but if the other person's goals are inconsistent with yours, then a conflict exists.

Conflict Styles

All of the preceding characteristics are present in any conflict. Yet
regardless of our gender, our culture, or any other factors at work, we are

all unique individuals who will react to conflict in our own way. In fact we might react differently in different situations. In class you might accept the grade received on an exam, even if you believe it to be incorrect, without confronting the instructor. At home you might argue with your father when you believe your assigned chores are more time-consuming than those assigned to your brother. The way we react in a situation where we have a conflict with someone is called our **conflict style**. There are five conflict styles that we might use depending on the person or situation involved; direct aggression, concealed aggression, passiveness, nonassertion, and assertion.

1. Direct Aggression. Aggressive individuals seem to take no notice of the goals of others. They are very focused on their own wants and desires, and attempt to satisfy them without regard to others' feelings or responses. The aggressive conflict style uses a direct physical or verbal attack. Often when you are in a conflict with someone who is aggressive, the person is hostile and angry. People who are aggressive like to choose solutions for others and let them know they are in control. Aggressive people leave others feeling confused, frustrated, and manipulated. In fact, if these people win an argument it is usually through manipulation. For example, a bully is an aggressive individual who manipulates anything or anyone to achieve her desired goal. She is intent on winning the "game" and will move or "manipulate" the players in any verbal or nonverbal way she deems necessary to get what she wants.

2. Concealed Aggression. This is an odd behavior. Inwardly, those who use this conflict style are just like directly aggressive people, because they focus on their own desires. They will attempt to gain them, but not through direct manipulation. These people use games that drive other people crazy! Let's say you are mad at your significant other because you have repeatedly asked him to take out the garbage and he keeps telling you he will do it later. If you were directly aggressive, you would scream and yell until he took out the garbage. But if you used concealed aggression, you would smile or nod, or even say "Oh don't worry about it." Then you might go outside and put the garbage behind his car so he would run over it in the morning. This type of "game" is manipulative and sends the message that you are in control. It often takes the other person awhile to figure it out, if he figures it out at all. People who use concealed aggression to deal with conflict situations choose solutions that make them feel they are in control. However, they make sure that the other person is caught off guard because that is part of the "game." Concealed aggressors leave others feeling frustrated, and once they finally figure out what has happened, they also feel like they've been used.

3. **Passiveness.** This is a behavior that a colleague of ours calls "the doormat." People who use this conflict style let everybody "wipe their feet all over them!" Rather than make a big deal out of something, these people simply give in and go along with what others want. The passive individual matches his goals to that of the group. Passive people use **accommodation** to put other people's needs ahead of their own, and they are often taken advantage of. It isn't that passive people necessarily want to be used by others; it's just that when faced with a conflict they choose the path of least resistance. They are unwilling or unable to express their thoughts, feelings, or opinions. Sometimes passive people choose this behavior if they know that the conflict is short-lived. Other times they may choose this behavior because they are afraid of being publicly humiliated or physically harmed for not going along with others. Regardless of why people choose a passive conflict style, others view them with disrespect, guilt, frustration, or anger. If a passive person wins an argument it is probably through sheer luck or the charity of others.

4. **Nonassertion.** People who attempt to resolve conflict by withholding their thoughts, opinions, or feelings on a topic at hand are using **nonassertion.** Although at first glance this behavior may seem to mimic that of the passive individual, there is one major difference. Nonassertive people withhold their opinion because they lack the confidence or skill to communicate their thoughts effectively. Where the passive individual will let others choose for them, the nonassertive person will use avoidance or indirect communication to deal with conflict.

Nonassertive individuals who use **avoidance** physically steer clear of the problem. When a conflict arises, they take off. They lack the skill and confidence to deal with problems, so avoidance is the path they choose. They may change the subject, joke, deny the issue, or walk way when you attempt to resolve conflict.

Nonassertive individuals who use **indirect communication** try to apply strategies that will soften the blow of any problem. They will hint, communicate in a roundabout fashion, or give clues, but never approach the situation in a straightforward manner. For example, if this type of person wants you to leave, rather than coming right out and asking you, he will yawn, look at his watch, or remark how fast the time has gone by today! He believes he is helping you to "save face" and everyone looks good. The problem with indirect communicators is that you never really know what they are trying to communicate!

Nonassertive individuals leave other people feeling confused. We never know how they really feel about an issue because they do not take a stand. Rather than avoid the issue altogether, they confuse us by adding irrelevant comments or behaviors. If they win an argument, it is because the other person involved has given up due to pure frustration.

5. *Assertion.* When you use assertive behavior, you take into account the other person's needs as well as your own. You have goals, but so does your partner in any conflict. For a relationship to remain strong both individuals must come away from a conflict feeling like they have reached a mutual understanding. This is the goal of assertive individuals. This style requires tact, sensitivity, and non-defensive communication. People who approach conflict by being assertive are looking for a positive solution to a conflict so that everybody "wins." Assertive people know that if the outcome of a disagreement isn't mutually satisfying, then the conflict is not really resolved. These people use direct confrontation and take responsibility for their own feelings and opinions. Although assertion is the best conflict style for most situations, not everyone will be receptive to its use. Directly aggressive individuals will still try to control assertive people, and passive individuals may still give in, but this method usually leaves both parties feeling respected, and both parties come out ahead in the long term.

In any situation, the importance of the conflict and who is involved will determine which conflict style you use. No one can make that decision but you. Since assertive behavior is honest and straightforward, this behavior may seem to be the most effective in conflict situations. Unfortunately, it isn't that simple. An effective communicator must analyze the situation and apply the behavior that will work for *all* the people involved. Just remember that aggressive behavior usually results in a defensive climate. A defensive climate is not conducive to reaching a solution. On the other hand, you may find yourself in a situation where you have attempted a number of ways to get cooperation and have received none. Not only won't the other party cooperate, she doesn't even listen to you. The most effective style in this case may be aggression. In dealing with some people, you need to "get in their face" before they pay attention or realize that what you are saying is important.

In other situations being passive is not only the most effective way of handling the situation, it is also the safest. There are risks involved in many conflict situations. Sometimes we need to be brave and take the risk if the situation is to improve. However, no one is suggesting that you put yourself in real danger. Passive conflict styles are appropriate if the other person might become violent either physically or verbally. Being passive is also an effective conflict style in situations where you disagree philosophically, politically, or religiously with someone. In other words, there are times, when for very good reasons, you may choose not to make your views be heard.

As you have continued to study communication, you probably have realized that there usually isn't a "right" answer as to exactly what you should do to be effective. All communication situations are different and need to be approached as unique. Conflict is no different. Remember, conflict exists until a solution is found that all parties can accept. There are several approaches you can try to find resolutions to conflict.

 Activity for Further Understanding

Conflict Styles

The purpose of this exercise is to further investigate how the five conflict styles affect communication. Read the following scenario and decide how you would handle the conflict if your conflict style were:

1. Direct Aggression
2. Concealed Aggression
3. Passiveness
4. Nonassertion
5. Assertion

You are seventeen and the only person in a group of friends who has a car. [c]oncert that you and your friends would like to attend is scheduled in a [nea]rby city. Since you are the only one with a consistent means of [trans]portation, you are often the person who drives your friends when they [want] to do something. Your friends rarely offer to give you gas money. Your [friend]s have decided you should be the person to stand in line to get concert [ticket]s for all of them. You assume that your friends will reimburse you for the [cost] of the tickets. You purchase the tickets, and between the time the [arrang]ements are made and the night of the concert, one member of the group [decide]s not to attend. The person who has canceled hasn't paid you for his [ticket a]nd doesn't mention doing so when he cancels.

[Ap]ply each style to this situation. What outcome would occur for each [sty]le? Which conflict style appears to be the most effective way of [sol]ving the problem? Be sure to explain and support your decision.

[Exp]lain why a solution to the problem might be found, but conflict [bet]ween you and your friend might exist. Hint: remember how each [style] makes the other party feel.

[If you] were really in this situation, which conflict style would you most [likely] use?

Approaches to Conflict

As we discussed before, when we are involved in a conflict there are several factors at work. Due to our emotional state and personal stake in the outcome of a conflict, we frequently don't approach the situation logically. If we are also involved in a power struggle to achieve our own desired outcome, disaster can occur. We've just looked at personal conflict styles and now we will look at four ways people attempt to resolve conflict in their lives. They are: I win, you lose; we both lose; we compromise; and let's agree.

I Win, You Lose

This approach may be most people's first choice to solving a conflict. Regardless of your conflict style, this is the style of resolution in which a conflict must have a winner and a loser. It is a power struggle that doesn't allow for the other person's needs or desires. People who use this type of conflict resolution see it as having only two possible outcomes. Either I get my way or you get yours. The assumption is, someone wins, and someone loses.

This approach to conflict resolution frequently involves threats, either stated or implied. Parents often use this approach with their children: you either do what I tell you to do, or you will be grounded. Bosses use it with employees: either you do the job I give you, or you're fired. It is used when we have a dispute over property, money, or other areas that are covered by law: either you fix my car, or I'll sue you.

Many of the ways we, as U.S. citizens, constitutionally resolve our differences are through the win–lose approach. The statement, majority rules, is a perfect example of this style in action. Electing a politician, voting on a referendum, or passing bills, all involve this form of power-laden conflict resolution. The majority wins, and the minority loses.

Whatever the specific behavior, the ultimate outcome is the same. If I can convince you that I am more powerful than you, I will come out on top, a winner. I may exert this power because I can affect your financial standing or because I am physically stronger than you. I may have more power because I can get more people to agree with me. I might have more power because I know you well and can make your life miserable. The point is, if you give in, you are admitting I am in some way stronger and more powerful than you. I win, and for whatever reason, you lose.

Notice that the desired outcome of resolving a conflict with this approach is to get your way. It is to show your opponent you are right or better. It is a game where only one person or side can win. It is rarely about solving the problem. Since this style is manipulative it is not the most effective way of handling conflict. However, there are times when this method *should* be used. Only one person or team can win a game. If a company is filling only one position, then only one person can get the job. If a child is running out in the street, a parent will need to intervene. Most conflicts, however, aren't really resolved with this method. You may win the battle but lose the war. You almost certainly will have to face this conflict again somewhere down the road. If you have a winner, you have someone who is considered "the loser." Losers usually fight back. They may wait until the conflict arises again, but directly or indirectly they will probably not only try to get even, they'll try to get ahead.

We Both Lose

You may be asking yourself why anyone would choose to resolve conflict by becoming a loser. The answer is that no one *chooses* to lose. This approach to conflict resolution usually results from two people with equal power attempting to win. They argue and present their views, but don't listen to each other. They forget that their purpose is to find a solution to the problem, not to become king of the hill. In this type of power struggle nothing is accomplished. Deadlines aren't met. Disastrous consequences aren't averted. In other words, nobody wins, everybody loses.

This approach probably is used more frequently than you think. A child wants to go to a friend's to play and the parent insists that he has to clean his room before he can go. The child whines or promises to do it after he comes back home. The parent asserts authority and says, "Either clean your room or you are grounded for the rest of the week." The child says, "I'm leaving" and starts out the door. The parent retrieves the child. They both stare at each other; they have come to a stalemate. Nobody has won. The child says, "I'm going to my room" and slams the door. The parent yells back, "Fine, you aren't going anywhere anyway!" The child loses because he doesn't get to play at his friend's *and* he's grounded. The parent loses because the bedroom still isn't clean and isn't likely to be. The same kind of power struggle results in our nation's capital when partisan politics becomes the issue rather than effecting legislation that will best help the country. It happens daily in big and small ways. When we are in conflict with someone who is as determined as we are to get his or her way, we are in a situation that most likely will end with both parties being losers.

Let's Compromise

All Tracey's life she has been told, by well-meaning people, that to get ahead in the world she needed to learn how to compromise. Every time she looked up the word compromise in the dictionary she'd find something similar to "an agreement arrived at when both parties make concessions." It has always seemed to her that to compromise meant two people agreed to something neither wanted. If I want to paint the room blue and you want to paint it yellow, do we take a little of each to compromise and paint the room green? Did either of us want to paint it green? No, but in order to arrive at a solution we agreed to give up part of our choice as long as the same sacrifice was made by the other party. Compromising can be a choice made by both parties to resolve a disagreement, so *something* can be accomplished, yet the compromise is a solution neither party wanted. Compromise often results from an attempt by each party to get at least part of her own way, because it is better than losing. Rather than walk away from a stalemate, one or both parties may attempt to initiate this approach to conflict.

Compromising is a frequently used method of conflict resolution. Our bicameral legislature was established due to compromise. States with low populations wanted to be represented equally with highly populated states. The states with the large populations wanted to be represented by population. Consequently, we have a House of Representatives and a Senate. On the surface this looks like the compromise resulted in both parties getting what they wanted. A closer look shows the desire of both small and large states was to gain power (remember, states were almost sovereign powers in the early days of the union). Neither really accomplished their goal. Was this famous compromise an effective way of resolving the problem? Most historians believe that compromise was needed to unite all the states under a federal government. On the other hand, look at all the redundancy at work when the House and the Senate have to approve bills. Think of the money spent on salaries for senators and representatives, their staffs, office expenses, and so forth. Just because a compromise works doesn't necessarily mean it is the *best* way to resolve the conflict.

Let's bring a compromise closer to home. Suppose both you and your spouse work. You own a six-room house that needs to be cleaned on a regular basis. Your spouse thinks you should do half of the cleaning. You, of course, believe she should do all of it. So, you decide to compromise. In fact, both of you agree to divide it evenly. Each will be responsible for cleaning three rooms. Six divided by two equals three. Pretty fair, a good compromise and solution to the conflict, right? Suppose you are to clean the kitchen, bathroom, and family room. Your spouse is to clean the master bedroom, guest bedroom (rarely used), and the dining room (you only eat in there on special occasions). This compromise is obviously numerically equal, but it isn't really equal. You have to clean the most-used (i.e., dirty) rooms while your spouse gets only one room that is used daily (the master bedroom). You can probably predict that the same conflict will arise again in just a few months, if not sooner. Compromise didn't really resolve the conflict!

If the conflict isn't that important to you, you can't seem to find another way to solve the problem, or you stand to lose more if you don't compromise, then this type of resolution might be the best to use. However, even though we use compromise frequently and even recommend it to others, it may not be the most effective way to resolve conflict.

Let's Agree

Finding a mutually agreed upon, equally satisfying solution to a conflict is the ideal way to resolve conflict. This method results in both parties being happy and pleased. They not only find a solution to the problem, but actually resolve their conflict by agreeing. Nice, you say, but it doesn't happen much in real life. It probably happens more than you realize. Many people can reach a consensus. In a consensus, a solution is found that is mutually satisfying. There are no losers in a consensus. The solution is developed by both parties, giving each ownership in the outcome. Believing they have been equal partners in resolving the problem, they work hard to make the solution work. This approach to conflict resolution is called the win–win approach. In contract negotiations or in situations where problem orientation is used (a supportive behavior discussed in chapter 9), this type of conflict resolution ends with "let's agree."

Just as there are times when compromise may seem the best choice to resolve a conflict, there are more times when consensus is the best choice. Sometimes none of these methods will work, and you must agree to drop the issue. That was the case for Mary and her husband for a recurring problem they had every spring and summer. During this time, Mary hit the road looking for yard sales and Dale hit the links at the golf course. The problem was money. Dale said she spent too much at yard sales, while Mary contended he spent way too much on golf. This same conflict arose every year just like the spring flowers; it kept coming back. After several unsuccessful attempts at resolving this problem, they agreed to disagree. The tension and arguments it was causing simply weren't worth it. Now Dale says, "I'm going to play golf," and Mary says, "I'm off to the sales." That's it. There is no fighting, no recrimination, no guilt trips. They have let it go and have given it a rest. They have agreed to disagree. Sometimes this is the only method that works!

Conclusion

We, your authors, know about conflict. Over the years we have personally been involved in more conflicts than we care to remember. We've tried all the conflict resolutions presented here. We've tried to win and have won. We've tried to win and have lost. However, the conflicts where both we and our partners reached an agreement through consensus were the most satisfying. For the rest of your life you will be facing conflict. You can approach it with dread and fear, you can be resentful, or you can blame the world for your misfortune. Better yet, you can approach each potential conflict situation with confidence in yourself and in the other person to be able to find a solution. You can regard these temporary hassles as part of the natural order of things, providing you with an opportunity to use your skills of survival. The choice is yours. All we ask is that you be responsible for the choices you make and the results of those choices.

DISCUSSION QUESTIONS

1. This chapter states that conflict can be beneficial. Agree or disagree with this statement and provide support for your belief through personal examples.

2. Identify your own most frequently used conflict style. Give at least two examples that led you to this conclusion.

3. Describe a situation you have been involved in where an attempt at winning actually led to both parties losing. Be sure to include information about what occurred that resulted in this outcome.

4. Using a conflict in your life, attempt to arrive at a consensus. What is the outcome? Are both parties satisfied?

5. Are you currently involved in a conflict that might best be handled by agreeing to disagree and let it be? If so, what benefits can you see to using this approach?

KEY TERMS

accommodation

assertion

avoidance

concealed aggression

conflict

conflict style

direct aggression

indirect communication

nonassertion

passiveness

The Susan and Jason Saga

If this were a fairy tale, we'd end this book with, "and they lived happily ever after." Jason and Susan would be riding off into the sunset never to experience a communication problem again. This isn't a fairy tale, and while Jason and Susan are fictitious characters, their communication problems are real. We've used them to help show how communication misunderstandings occur in our daily lives. We must continually be aware that the messages we are sending may not be those received. Communication is dynamic and ever changing. We can never "rest" if we want our communication with others to be effective. Effective communication requires constant awareness and significant skills. Skills we hope the *Key to Survival* has helped you learn.

Susan smiled as she watched Jason throw the ball to their seven-year-old grandson Mark. Mark wanted to be a baseball player when he grew up. To Susan it seemed practically yesterday that Mark's dad, their son Michael, had declared his own intention of being a big league pitcher. It hadn't happened, he'd actually become a teacher at the local high school, but he did coach Little League.

Jason looked up and saw Susan standing at the kitchen window smiling. He wondered why she was smiling, but assumed it meant she was happy. Jason wanted Susan to be happy. He wouldn't say the last 35 years of their marriage had always been smooth. In fact, over the years there had been more misunderstandings than he cared to remember. He'd even found himself sleeping on the sofa a few times in the past. These problems were almost always caused by a lack of communication, or misinterpretation of what the other person had meant, but they'd always been able to work things out. If there was one thing they both had learned, it was to listen and keep the lines of communication open.

Susan called to Jason and Mark telling them lunch was ready. Jason replied, "We'll be there in a little while." An hour later, Susan wasn't smiling as she put lunch in the refrigerator. Jason and Mark hadn't come inside to eat, despite her telling them to several times. She knew they'd heard her, weren't they listening? She knew after all these years that Jason's "a little while" was a lot longer than what she considered "a little while," but continuing to play ball when she'd taken the time to fix a nice lunch must mean he took her for granted. Men!

As Jason put the equipment away in the garage, he couldn't help but see that storage was getting out of hand. He and Susan had better clean it up or they wouldn't be able to park the car. Why did Susan keep all this old stuff? It just cluttered up the garage. He'd suggest they go through it all this afternoon, and take the things they didn't need to the local homeless shelter. Maybe, if they finished early enough, they'd be able to go out to dinner. What a great idea, thought Jason. I'll make late reservations at The Station and surprise Susan. We haven't been there in years, and Susan loved surprises. Pleased with his plan to get the garage cleaned out and surprise Susan with dinner at "their place," Jason went inside to eat lunch. He was surprised to see that the kitchen table was empty.

"I thought you said lunch was ready," said Jason.

"That was an hour ago," replied Susan, "You obviously didn't care that I had it ready, so now you can just get it yourself. Mark is eating in the family room watching TV."

"What do you mean I don't care?" Susan gives no verbal response to his question, but from her nonverbal behavior, Jason can tell she is angry. He decides to change the subject while he fixes himself a plate and heats it up in the microwave. "I've been thinking that we should get rid of all that junk in the garage. Let's do it this afternoon."

"Junk? I cleaned the garage out last month. Everything else needs to be stored in there unless you want to get rid of all those tools you insisted on buying and never use."

Jason frowns, then takes a deep breath. He doesn't want to argue. He realizes he shouldn't have waited so long before coming in to eat, because Susan is now defensive. "Susan, I'm sorry we didn't come in when you first called. Let me make it up to you. Would you have dinner with me at The Station tonight?" asks Jason.

Susan, who is very angry at this point, says, "You want to take me to the train station for dinner? What kind of apology is that?!"

"Oh no," thought Jason as he remembered a similar conversation over 35 years ago. "Here we go again!"

Glossary

accommodation. Conflict style in which you give in to the demands of others.

affect display. Cues used to indicate an emotional response; add power and reinforcement to the spoken word.

aggression. Conflict style that uses any and all means available to manipulate another person to gain what you want; often involves physical and verbal attacks.

apathy. Reacting as if nothing has happened; a *flee mechanism.*

artifacts. Form of nonverbal communication that includes jewelry, glasses, watches, etc.; subcategory of clothing.

assertion. Conflict style that requires you to take responsibility for your thoughts; it requires tact, sensitivity, and nondefensive communication; the most effective *conflict resolution* style.

assimilation. Comparing new information with prior information already stored in our heads.

assumptions. Beliefs that we hold to be true, that we accept as true without needing proof.

authority figures. People whom we allow to control us; parents, significant others, etc.

avoidance. Physically steering clear of a problem.

axioms. Statements that we accept as truth.

benefit. Perceived gain from engaging in self-disclosure.

biases. The inclination to be in favor of or against something; based on our *assumptions.*

certainty. Acting as if you are always right; *defense-producing behavior.*

channel. Medium through which a message travels.

climate. Environment in which we attempt to communicate; can be positive or negative.

communication. Process of thinking and feeling, and receiving and conveying messages to ourselves and others in a manner that brings ideas and people together.

compensation. Changing the subject or bringing up another topic we can discuss successfully; a *flee mechanism.*

173

conflict. Term that encompasses everything from a small disagreement to all-out war; it is inevitable and cannot be avoided; a struggle over something.

conflict style. Way in which we react or respond in a conflict situation.

connotative. Meaning connected to a word by an individual based on his feelings and experiences.

control. Acting like the boss, telling others what to do; *defense-producing behavior.*

corpus callosum. Bundle of nerve fibers that connect the two hemispheres of the brain, allowing messages to travel from side to side.

cross-communication. Using our own gender style to communicate with the opposite gender, resulting in our message being interpreted in a way opposite to that which we intended.

decoding. Process of turning a message back into mental images or symbols.

defense mechanism. Way we tend to react when we are under attack; we will fight or flee.

defense-producing behaviors. Six actions, categorized by psychologist Jack Gibb, commonly perceived as being the cause or motivating event that results in people becoming defensive.

defensiveness. The feeling we experience that causes us to take actions to protect our presenting, public image.

deliberate listening. Listening for a very specific reason.

denotative. Dictionary meaning of a word.

description. Stating thoughts and opinions for what they are, an opinion; a supportive behavior.

displacement. Act of avoiding someone involved in the situation, and acting out to someone else; a *flee mechanism.*

emblems. Form of nonverbal cues (language) that uses gesturing to communicate; usually agreed upon by a culture or group.

empathic listening. Listening process that uses *empathy;* a *supportive behavior.*

empathy. Process of understanding the whole message by attempting to experience not only how someone is responding but why the person is responding that way; concept of putting yourself in someone else's shoes; also a supportive behavior.

encoding. Process of turning mental images into symbols.

equality. Basis of treating others as equals; a *supportive behavior.*

euphemism. Substitution for a word that we find too graphic or upsetting.

evaluation. Passing judgment; a *defense-producing behavior.*

external noise. Distraction outside our body that interferes with the listening process.

fantasy. Retreating into your own thoughts or daydreams where you are in control of the situation; a *flee mechanism.*

feedback. Constant exchange of messages that provides message verification; a response to a message.

fight mechanisms. Used when trying to defend our public image; retaliation against any injury; usually a verbal accusation or physical attack.

filling in the gaps. Poor listening habit of making up information to fill in gaps with details we missed.

flee mechanisms. Used when we choose to avoid a fight and attempt to run away as a means of defense.

gender communication. Communication between men and women.

group. People who share similar activities or interests.

habits. Behavior patterns acquired by frequent repetition.

identity management. Presenting ourselves differently to different people.

illustrators. Signals that help clarify or emphasize spoken words; a form of nonverbal cue created by gesturing.

indirect communication. Hinting or giving clues but never a straightforward message.

inflated language. Words that make a situation or object seem more favorable or desirable.

internal noise. Distraction to the listening process that occurs inside your body.

interpersonal communication. Transmission and exchange of ideas, which occurs between and among people.

intimate space. Distance of about zero to twelve inches; can include touching or skin contact.

intrapersonal communication. Thoughts, ideas, memories that are our internal communication.

jargon. Industry-specific words that have been developed for use within and among a group.

language. Written or spoken system of symbols that is rule guided.

lifestyle choices. Decisions we make based on our everyday experiences, including group memberships and our value system.

mass communication. Communication that occurs between thousands of people; often accomplished through media such as television or radio.

message. Idea that you want the other person to understand.

message overload. Process of being overwhelmed with thoughts or concerns; interferes with the listening process.

neutrality. Ignoring others, failing to respond; a *defense producing behavior.*

noise. Any force that distracts from *hearing* or *listening.*

nonassertion. Withholding our thoughts or feelings.

nonverbal communication. Any communication that does not use language.

nonverbal cues. Behaviors that signal or convey meaning to others without the use of words.

opaque rule. Rule developed by the authors of this text that suggests doing unto others as they would have done unto themselves.

oxytocin. Known as the "bonding" chemical, high levels cause aggression.

paralanguage. Voice tone and pitch; volume that accompanies language; the manner in which we say a word.

paraphrasing. Repeating, in your own words, what you believe the speaker has said.

parents. Persons who raised you from infancy; see also *authority figures.*

participatory listening. Listening process that repeats what a speaker has said through the use of paraphrasing.

passiveness. Conflict style in which you allow others to use you without putting up a defense; becoming the "doormat of the world."

peers. People who are approximately our same age and have the same economic and social status.

perceived self. What we honestly believe to be true about our self.

perception process. Categorizing and labeling those events that we experience; often called a "first impression."

personal environment. Collective experiences we have had beginning the day we were born, which shape our feelings and thoughts.

personal space. Distance of about twelve inches to three feet that surrounds our body; our personal "bubble."

physical noise. Distraction to the listening process that occurs when our body is affected by physical problems or defects.

physiological factors. Major group of influencing factors in the perception process; these factors include the five senses and any other physical body elements.

prejudice. Irrational feeling of hostility or dislike directed at a group or individual.

preoccupation. Noise caused by your own internal thoughts; your intrapersonal communication.

presenting self. Person we show to others; what we want them to believe about us; also called the public self.

problem orientation. Taking into account the other person's feelings and ideas and incorporating them as part of the solution; a *supportive behavior.*

projection. Placing offense back on our accuser; a *fight mechanism.*

provisionalism. Allowing the other person to state his or her beliefs, reasons, and feelings even if they cannot be incorporated into the solution; a *supportive behavior.*

proxemics. How we use or move through space to communicate a message.

psychological factors. Major group of influencing factors in the perception process; mental choices that we make, such as social and lifestyle choices.

psychological noise. Internal mental distraction or preoccupation.

public communication. Communication that occurs between a roomful of 20 or more people.

public space. Distance of about 15 feet or more; usually the greatest amount of space between people.

rationalization. Giving a logical but essentially untrue explanation of why we did something; a *fight mechanism.*

reciprocal defensiveness. What is done by one to the other is done and returned by the other; when one responds defensively to the defensiveness of another.

reciprocity. Reason for disclosing; the concept of "you scratch my back and I'll scratch yours," encouraging others to share their disclosures in exchange for us sharing ours.

referent group. Group of peers we refer to in order to gauge how well we are doing in society.

reflected appraisal. Influence on our self-concept that occurs when we accept the judgments of other individuals, society as a whole (see also *social norms*), or the media; opinions from others used as a mirror in which we see ourselves.

regression. Choosing to act like a child; a *flee mechanism.*

repression. Trying to avoid by pretending the action didn't take place or by disavowing any connection to it; a *flee mechanism.*

retreat (physically and mentally). Removing ourselves as a means of coping; a *flee mechanism.*

reversal. Trying to "reverse" or change another's opinion of us; a *flee mechanism.*

sarcasm. Use of tone or pitch to attack our opposition; a *fight mechanism.*

selective listening. Choosing or selecting parts of a message, only those parts we want to listen to.

self-catharsis. Reason for disclosing; a way to clear the air and get something "off your chest."

self-clarification. Reason for disclosing; uses others as a sounding board, painting a clearer picture of something in our own mind.

self-concept. Beliefs a person holds to be true about himself or herself; what we think about ourselves.

self-disclosure. Act of deliberately revealing to another person your intimate thoughts, feelings, and experiences as they occur.

self-esteem. Emotional response to our self-concept; how we feel about who we are; how much we value our self.

self-fulfilling prophecy. Strongly held belief that makes the outcome of some event more likely to happen.

self-validation. Reason for disclosing; proving to yourself that your thoughts are correct.

serotonin. Brain chemical that produces a calming effect when released into the bloodstream.

significant others. People with whom we spend a great deal of time and whose opinions we seek; see also *authority figures.*

small group communication. Interpersonal communication that occurs between as few as 3 people and as many as 20 people.

social comparison. How we judge (compare) ourselves to the people we are involved with and to broader society as a whole.

social control. Disclosing only information that presents our strengths and repressing information about our weaknesses or liabilities.

social norms. Unwritten laws of society that we are expected to follow in order to be accepted by society.

social situations. Experiences and encounters with others that have an effect on the perception process; these situations include elements such as religion, family heritage, cultural background, and economic status.

social space. Distance of about four to fifteen feet; usually used in social spaces.

society. Organized group in which we live and function.

speaking/thinking rate. Ability to understand speech at a rate four to five times faster than the average person can actually speak.

spontaneity. Spur of the moment honesty in communication; a *supportive behavior.*

stage hogging. Poor listening habit of interrupting another person so you can express your own views or opinions.

stereotype. Preconceived idea about a person or situation; often based on assumptions and past experiences that we wrongly use to judge others.

strategy. Act of manipulating another to achieve your goal; a *defense-producing behavior.*

superiority. Acting better than someone else; a *defense-producing behavior.*

supportive behaviors. Six actions categorized by psychologist Jack Gibb that, when used, tend to lessen the likelihood of defensiveness and send a message of support and acceptance.

surface information. Straightforward, topical, and verifiable information; information that is commonly known by others.

symbols. Words or gestures that represent a mental image.

territoriality. Claiming ownership of the space around us.

verbal communication. Using language (words) to communicate.

Index

Accommodation, 162
Affect displays, 40
Aggression, 161
Ambiguity, 29
Apathy, 147
Appearance, 34
Artifacts, 35
Assertion, 163
Assimilation, 55
Assumptions, 54–55
Attending, 50
Auditory perception, 128–129
Authority figures, 66–68
Avoidance, 162
Axioms of communication, 9–12

Biases, 54–55
Body language, 34–35, 40
Brain chemicals/brain functions,
    105–108, 110

Catharsis, 85, 91
Certainty, 150
Channels, 15, 40–41
Clarification, 22, 29–30
Climate, 149
Clothing, 35
Communication
    anticipational vs. impromptu, 29
    avoiding value judgments about, 9–10
    axioms of, 9–12
    circular process of, 16
    definition of, 13
    dynamic and essential, 11–12
    effectiveness quiz, 75–76

gender differences in, 102–123. *See
    also* Gender communication
learned skill of, 12
model of, 14–18
mutual process of, 12
nonverbal, 32–45. *See also* Nonver-
    bal communication
reasons for, 6–9
time and, 10–11
verbal, 20–30. *See also* Verbal com-
    munication
Compensation, 147
Compromise, 166–167
Concealed aggression, 161
Conflict
    characteristics of, 159–160
    definition of, 157
    factors contributing to, 158–159
    resolution, approaches to, 165–168
    styles of, 160–164
Confusion, reduction of, 29
Connotative meanings, 24–25
Consensus, 168
Control, 149–150
Corpus callosum, 107
Cross-communication, 114–116,
    117–120
Culture
    challenges to self-disclosure, 93
    conflict management and, 158–159
    influence on gender communica-
        tion, 112–113
    influence on perception, 134–135
    influence on self-concept, 70–71
    nonverbal cues dependent on, 42

Decoding, 16
Defense mechanisms, 146, 147–149
Defensiveness
    behaviors that eliminate, 150–153
    causes of, 149–150
    conflict and, 159
    definition of, 145–146
    presenting self and, 146
    reciprocal, 146, 149
Deliberate listening, 60
Denotative meanings, 24–25
Description, 151
Direct aggression, 161
Displacement, 147
Distance and territoriality, 36–37
Dyadic self-disclosure, 91–92

Ego needs, 8
Emblems, 39
Emotions, 92–93
Empathic communication, 119
Empathic listening, 60–61
Empathy, 151
Encoding, 15–17
Environmental management cues,
    35–37
Equality, 152
Euphemism, 26–27
Evaluation, 22, 50, 149
External environment, 35, 37, 56
External noise, 17, 56

Fantasy, 148
Feedback, 16, 97
Fight mechanisms, 147
Filling in the gaps, 57
First impressions, 42–43, 127
Flee mechanisms, 147–149

Gender
    challenges to self-disclosure, 93–94
    conflict management and, 158
    nonverbal cues and, 43–44
    societal expectations and self-con-
        cept, 69–70
Gender communication
    avoiding problems in, 117–120
    cross-communication, 114–120
    definition of, 104

effective, tips for, 120–123
    nature vs. nurture debate, 106–114
    opaque rule in, 117–120
    problems with, 114–117
    styles of, 104–105, 111–112
Gestures/gesturing, 39, 43
Gibb Categories of Defensive and Sup-
    portive Behaviors, 151–153
Gossip, 53
Group membership, 69
Gustatory perception, 129–130

Habits, 52–55
Hearing
    auditory perception and, 128–129
    definition of, 14, 49
    in the listening process, 49–50
Hinting, 90
Honesty, 91
Hormones, and gender communica-
    tion, 108–110

Identity management, 87
Illustrators, 39
Indirect communication, conflict style
    of, 162
Inflated language, 27–28
Internal noise, 17, 56
Interpersonal communication
    categories of, 13
    definition of, 9
    listening in. *See* Listening
    verbal. *See* Verbal communication
Intimate space, 35
Intrapersonal communication, 13, 56

Jargon, 26

Labeling, 22
Language
    arbitrary nature of, 24–25
    characteristics of, 23–25
    conscious nature of, 23–24
    importance of, 21–22
    management cues/paralanguage, 38
    misuse of, 25–28
    singular process of, 24
    substitution of nonverbal cues for,
        39

symbolic nature of, 25
    uses of, 22–23
Lifestyle choices, influence on perception, 134
Likert Scales, 138
Listening
    benefits of, 58–59
    cross-communication and, 120
    definition of, 49
    hearing vs.,14
    ineffective, costs of, 51–52
    ineffective, reasons for, 52–58
    process of, 49–51
    selective, 56
    styles of, 59–61
Lying, 89–90

Manipulation, 87–88, 90
Masking/withholding reactions, 90
Mass communication, 13
Media, 68, 113
Message, 15
Message overload, 57

Nature vs. nurture, 106–114
Neutrality, 150
Noise, 17–18, 56
Nonassertion, 162
Nonverbal communication
    arbitrary nature of, 41–42
    characteristics of, 40–42
    continuous nature of, 41
    definition of, 14, 33
    difficulties with, 42–44
    language management cues, 38
    suggestions for effective, 44–45
    through many channels, 40–41
    types of cues in, 33–38
    unconscious nature of, 40
    uses of, 39–40
Nonverbal cues
    environmental management, 35–37
    gender-related, 43–44
    self-presentation, 34–35
    verbal confirmation of, 45

Olfactory perception, 130
Opaque rule, 117–120
Oxytocin, 110

Paralanguage, 38, 41, 147
Paraphrasing, 61, 119
Parents, 66–67
Participatory listening, 60–61
Passiveness, 162
Peer pressure, 68–69
Perceived self vs. presenting self, 145–146
Perception
    auditory, 128–129
    challenges to process of, 138–140
    characteristics of, 136–137
    decreasing misunderstandings of, 140
    definition of, 127–128
    fatigue's influence on, 131–132
    gustatory, 129–130
    health's influence on, 132–133
    height and weight's influence on, 131
    hunger's influence on, 132
    nonverbal communication by appearance, 34
    olfactory, 130
    primary physiological influences on, 128–130
    psychological factors affecting, 133–136
    psychological factors influencing, 133
    secondary physiological influences on, 130–133
    tactile, 129
    temperature's influence on, 131
    visual, 128
    at work, 135
Personal environment, 14, 16–17
Personal space, 36
Physical/practical needs, 6–7
Prejudice, 55
Preoccupation, 56
Presenting self, 145–146, 148, 154
Problem orientation, 151
Projection, 147
Provisionalism, 152
Proxemics, 35–36
Public communication, 13
Public space, 36

Rationalization, 147
Reciprocal defensiveness, 146, 149

Reciprocity, 86
Referent groups, 68
Reflected appraisal, 66–67
Regression, 148
Regulating controls, 39
Relationships, 86–87
Repression, 148
Responding, 51
Retaining, 50
Retreat, 148
Reversal, 148

Sarcasm, 147
Selective listening, 56
Selective perception, 136
Self, 72, 74
Self-catharsis, 85
Self-clarification, 85–86, 91
Self-communication, 6–7, 13
Self-concept
    authority figures' influence on,
      66–68
    cultural influences on, 70–71
    definition of, 65
    formation of, 66–72
    gender expectations and, 69–70
    making positive changes in, 76–78
    peer pressure and, 68–69
    self-beliefs and, 71–72
    social comparisons and, 68–69
Self-disclosure
    challenges to, 92–94
    characteristics of, 90–92
    choice involved in, 84–85
    definition of, 83
    effective, technique for, 96–97
    facilitating, 96
    guidelines for, 94–96
    reasons for, 85–89
    unacceptable alternatives to, 89–90
Self-esteem
    definition of, 65
    ego needs and, 8
Self-fulfilling prophecy, 73, 76–77
Self-presentation cues, 34–35
Self-validation, 86, 91
Serotonin, 110
Significant others, as authority figures,
    67–68

Small group communication, 13
Social comparisons, 68–69
Social control, 87
Social needs, 7–8
Social situations, 133–134
Social space, 36
Society, 69–71, 133–134
Space, 35–37, 44
Speaking/thinking rate, 57
Spontaneity, 151
Stage hogging, 54
Stereotypes, 137
Strategy, 150
Superiority, 150
Supportive behaviors, 151
Surface information, 83
Survival needs, 6–8
Symbol(s). 15, 21, 25

Tactile perception, 129
Taste, 129–130
Territoriality, 36–37
Touch, 35, 43, 129
Truthfulness, 91

Value judgments, 9–10
Verbal communication
    definition of, 14, 21–22
    effective, suggestions for, 28–30
    language and. See Language
Verification, 23
Visual perception, 128
Voice, 38, 147

Women
    gender roles and self-concept of,
      69–70
    gender-specific characteristics of,
      115–117
    nonverbal cues of, 43–44
    self-disclosure and, 93–94
    tips for effective gender communi-
      cation, 121–123
Words. See also Language
    abuse of, 25–28
    reducing confusion and ambiguity
      through, 29
    as symbols, 25